Patterns *for* Prayer

Volume 3: September - December

Alvin VanderGriend

Love 2 Pray

PrayerShop Publishing

Terre Haute, Indiana

PrayerShop Publishing is the publishing arm of the Church Prayer Leaders Network. The Church Prayer Leaders Network exists to equip and inspire local churches and their prayer leaders in their desire to disciple their people in prayer and to become a "house of prayer for all nations." Its online store, prayershop.org, has more than 150 prayer resources available for purchase or download.

ISBN (Print): 978-1-970176-17-9

ISBN: (E-Book): 978-1-970176-18-6

Original contributors to this prayer guide include Edith Bajema, Dian Ginter, Joan Huyser-Honig, Don McCrory, Laurie Quist, Al Schaap, Mark Timmer, Alvin J. VanderGriend, and Jean Westenbroek.

TABLE OF CONTENTS

September 6
October 36
November 67
December 97

PREFACE

This book is designed to help you develop a meaningful and disciplined personal prayer life. I have heard people say, "I'd like to pray more, but after five minutes I run out of things to pray about." Most of us know what that's like. *Patterns for Prayer* is for all who have "run out of things to pray about."

Regular use of this prayer guide will help you

- learn to use the language of Scripture in prayer
- use all of the elements of prayer regularly
- claim the promises of God with confidence
- keep your thoughts from wandering during prayer
- pray expressively for friends and family
- release God's power and grace for your church and the kingdom of God
- develop the habit of praying for unsaved friends and acquaintances

You'll discover a weekly cycle in these pages as you pray for the leadership and ministries of your own local church. You'll pray about worship, church leaders, outreach ministries, church education, world missions, caregiving and fellowship, and financial stewardship.

This guide is meant to enlarge and deepen your prayer life. It is not intended to be the whole of it. Let these prayer suggestions trigger prayer expressions from your own heart. Where they do not fit, customize them to your own situation. Space is provided on each page for you to keep a record of further petitions and intercessions.

The Heidelberg Catechism reminds us that "God gives his grace and Holy Spirit only to those who pray continually and groan inwardly, asking God for these gifts and thanking him for them" (Q&A 116). I pray that you may do just that and, in so doing, find that your life is enriched as you grow in intimacy with God and receive a generous amount of his grace and Spirit.

—Alvin J. VanderGriend

SEPTEMBER 1

Personal Prayer

Praise the God of peace. Thank him for making available that "peace at all times and in every way" (2 Thess. 3:16). Confess ways in which you have added to an argument or refused to let God's peace be established between you and another person. Commit to being at peace with God and others by being both pure in heart and a peacemaker (Mt. 5:8-9). Ask God to spread the wholeness of his salvation through you.

For Your Family and Friends

Pray for any marriages or parent-child relationships among family and friends where God's peace is not being experienced right now. Ask God to help you know how and when to speak, be quiet, mediate, etc.

For the Church

Pray for the fellowship of your local church to be unhindered by strife and controversy. Ask God to also bring his peace to your denomination.

For the Kingdom

Pray for those who are peacemakers between nations in conflict. Ask God to prompt Christians to full involvement as peacemakers.

For the Unsaved

Pray that the willingness of Christians to resolve even difficult differences will be a brilliant display of God's love to the unsaved. Ask God to bring an unsaved friend into his family.

Prayer Pointer

"Front-line prayer meetings are battle stations in which the prayer warriors themselves are changed." —The Praying Church Sourcebook

SEPTEMBER 2

Personal Prayer

Praise God for his indescribable love. Thank God for loving you so much that he would sacrifice his own son. Confess ways you have not been generous with your love in response. Commit to offering even your very body as a living sacrifice, holy and pleasing to God (Rom. 12:1). Ask him to help you not to be conformed to the world but to be transformed by the renewing of your mind (12:2).

For Your Family and Friends

Pray for Christian friends and family members to stand true for God no matter the cost. Ask that they be filled with God's joy in the midst of sacrifices.

For the Church

Pray for believers being persecuted for righteousness. Ask God to help them remember the heavenly reward, enabling all to rejoice and be glad even in the face of insults and false accusations for the sake of Christ (Mt. 5:10-12).

For the Kingdom

Pray that Christians giving sacrificially will be irresistible evidence of the presence and power of God. Ask God to multiply these sacrifices for the extension of his kingdom.

For the Unsaved

Pray that God will give you opportunities to give of your time and resources to help an unsaved acquaintance. Ask God to help you continue to share his love in spite of possible opposition.

SEPTEMBER 3

Personal Prayer

This week, meditate on Psalm 42 each day. Today, praise God as the one who quenches your deepest spiritual thirst (42:1-2). Thank him for being the living water in your life. Confess times in your life when you've passed by God's streams of water and settled for Satan's stale pond instead. Commit yourself to quenching your thirst in the living God alone. Ask him to meet with you in prayer today.

For Your Family and Friends

Pray that your family will be a refreshing oasis of hospitality and warmth as you open yourselves to the needs of others.

For the Church

Do the members of your congregation thirst for God as they come to worship? Pray that they will. Pray also for God to prepare your own heart as you join with others in God's house this Sunday.

For the Kingdom

Pray for missionaries in many countries who share with hurting people not only the bread of life, but also cups of cold water in the name of Christ. Ask God's blessing on their labors.

For the Unsaved

Pray that your own thirst for a closer relationship with God might draw others to him. Ask God to get you out of the way so that they might see Jesus clearly and drink deeply of him.

Prayer Pointer

"Whether we like it or not, asking is the rule of the kingdom."—Charles H. Spurgeon

SEPTEMBER 4

Personal Prayer

Praise God for his constant presence with you every day. Thank him for always being near you even in times of extreme difficulty (Ps. 42:3). Confess those times when you've doubted God's loving presence. Commit yourself to seeking his face every morning in prayer and meditation. Ask God to go with you throughout this day.

For Your Family and Friends

Pray that believing members of your family will have a distinct sense of God's presence with them. Ask God to help them in times of distress.

For the Church

Pray for all the leaders in your congregation: your pastor, elders, deacons, ministry heads, and others who come to mind. Pray for God's obvious presence in their lives.

For the Kingdom

Ask God to provide the necessary funds for ministries dedicated to saving the lives of the unborn. Pray that believers will not lose heart in the battle against abortion.

For the Unsaved

Pray that the question "Where is your God?" might come home to an unbelieving friend or neighbor. Ask God to prepare you to speak a word of grace to that person.

SEPTEMBER 5

Personal Prayer

Praise God for the privilege of coming to him in worship and praise today. Give thanks with "shouts of joy and thanksgiving" (Ps. 42:4) for God's many benefits. Confess your occasional lack of enthusiasm in devotion. Commit yourself to "festive" times of personal worship. Ask God to meet with you on those occasions.

For Your Family and Friends

Ask that the devotional experiences of your family and friends will be characterized by joy. Pray that the Spirit will enliven their walk with God.

For the Church

Ask God to bless the work of outreach ministries in your neighborhood or city. Pray that they will be empowered as they seek to bring the gospel to needy people.

For the Kingdom

Pray for any in your congregation who are unemployed or underemployed. Ask God to provide the work and financial resources needed. Ask him to grant encouragement to these people—perhaps through you.

For the Unsaved

Pray that an unbelieving neighbor might be led to question your joy in serving the Lord and thus provide an opportunity for you to share your faith. Pray for eyes to see and ears to hear these divine encounters.

Prayer Pointer

"Prayer is a shield to the soul, a sacrifice to God, and a scourge for Satan."
—John Bunyan

SEPTEMBER 6

Personal Prayer

Praise God as the one who lifts your soul up from the depths of despair and discouragement (Ps. 42:5). Thank him for being your Savior and your God. Confess those times when you've chosen not to allow God to wipe away the tears of distress. Commit yourself to praising God every day for his tender mercies. Ask God to keep you from becoming downcast in your soul.

For Your Family and Friends

Pray for any close friends who struggle with depression or discouragement. Ask God to come close to them today and show them his marvelous love.

For the Church

Pray for the educational programs in your church. Thank God for those who write curriculum material. Intercede on behalf of teachers and helpers who instruct children and youth.

For the Kingdom

Intercede for Christian counseling agencies which help people find the healing light of Christ in the midst of a dark and dreary life. Pray that you will have greater compassion for those who suffer mental illness.

For the Unsaved

Ask God to cause many around the world today to "put their hope in God" (42:5) and thus be able to confess with believers in every land "my Savior and my God" (42:11).

SEPTEMBER 7

Personal Prayer

Praise God as the one who protects you from life's roaring waterfalls and waves (Ps. 42:7). Give thanks that even in the stormy times of life God is always near. Confess those times when you've questioned God's presence or doubted his protection. Commit yourself to staying by his side no matter what comes your way. Ask God to lead and guide you through the stormy as well as the calm seasons of life.

For Your Family and Friends

Pray for any teens among your family or acquaintances who are weathering the all-too-common storms of abuse, parental divorce, or suicide. Ask for God's grace.

For the Church

Thank God for the work and witness of missionaries around the world. Pray that they will go on the wings of a praying church back home. Intercede especially for world missionaries supported by your church.

For the Kingdom

Pray for revival in the church in North America. Ask God to raise up faithful pastors and teachers. Pray that the gods of secularism and materialism will be cast out of our church families.

For the Unsaved

Think of one person with whom you could develop a friendship. It might be someone you see at work, or on the bus, or in your neighborhood. Ask God to create opportunities for you to share your faith—and then be ready to do so!

SEPTEMBER 8

Personal Prayer

Praise God for his love, which is with you both night and day (Ps. 42:8). Give thanks for the songs of praise which God brings forth from you. Confess that you sometimes don't feel like reveling in God's love or singing his praises. Commit yourself to living every day in the light of that love. Ask God to continue directing his love toward you.

For Your Family and Friends

Pray for the older members of your family—parents, grandparents, aunts and uncles. Pray that their later years of life will be filled with health and vitality. Intercede for any who are failing physically or mentally.

For the Church

Thank God for fellowship opportunities your church provides. Pray that caregiving and fellowship will extend outward, too, so that the needs of those in your neighborhood might be met through your church family.

For the Kingdom

Pray for believers in the federal governments of both the U.S. and Canada. Thank God that he has placed his people in and near the seats of highest political power. Ask that they will be enabled to make a difference because they serve the Savior.

For the Unsaved

Ask God to "direct his love" to a particular friend or acquaintance who does not yet know Jesus. Pray for an opportunity to share your faith with that person. Keep that one in your prayers throughout this week.

SEPTEMBER 9

Personal Prayer

Praise God for all his many blessings to you in your life (Ps. 42:11). Thank him that he is your God and that there is nothing that can ruin your relationship with him. Confess that you don't always feel like praising God. Commit yourself to living in hope every day. Ask God to surround you with his presence—and then respond to him with praise.

For Your Family and Friends

Pray for the youngest members of your circle of family and friends. Intercede for any infants or toddlers. Ask God to bless them with good health, with safe surroundings, and with loving parents who will teach them to love the Lord.

For the Church

Pray for the financial giving in your church. Ask that those who give generously will receive their reward for faithful stewardship. Ask that there will be a spirit of generosity among the members.

For the Kingdom

Pray for those who have the gift of evangelism and who use it in various ways. Ask that the proclamation of the gospel in cities, towns, and rural areas will be met with a harvest of souls.

For the Unsaved

Think of a world map and pray for the harvest among the nations. Ask for breakthroughs in countries that have been particularly resistant to the gospel. Ask God to touch the lives of people in every country around the world today.

SEPTEMBER 10

Personal Prayer

Praise God as your mighty, protective, and loving Father. Thank him for adopting you as his own son or daughter and for making you heir to all the promises given in Scripture (Gal. 3:26-29). Confess those times you have forgotten who you are—a child of the Most High God. Commit yourself to remembering each day that you have been born into God's family and have "clothed yourself with Christ" (3:27). Ask God to help you understand and appreciate your complete inheritance in Jesus Christ (Eph. 1:18).

For Your Family and Friends

Pray that the fathers you know will be able to reflect the Father's love, compassion, and wisdom to their children, so that the entire family will grow to trust and love God.

For the Church

Ask God to help your congregation welcome its neighbors and those who may be different in skin color, culture, economic class, or nationality, celebrating that "you are all one in Christ Jesus" (Gal. 3:28).

For the Kingdom

Pray that Christians in warring or oppressive countries may be shining lights of justice and compassion toward those who are being shunned or harmed.

For the Unsaved

Ask your Father to draw his wayward sons and daughters into his growing family.

SEPTEMBER 11

Personal Prayer

Praise God as the one who holds out his arms to the world in welcoming love and invitation. Thank God for having intervened in your life to bring you to a growing knowledge of his love for you. Confess your sins of this past week, trusting in the power of Jesus' blood to reconcile you with God. Commit yourself to becoming more aware of God's outreaching love toward your neighbors and friends. Ask him to make you a minister of reconciliation (2 Cor. 5:18-21).

For Your Family and Friends

Pray for those families who have been struggling with bitterness or alienation, asking God to bring reconciliation into their homes.

For the Church

Ask God to give the leaders of your church and denomination the ability to be effective "ambassadors of Christ," bringing a message of reconciliation to their communities. Pray also for unity and forgiveness where there are rifts in leadership.

For the Kingdom

Pray for reconciliation among foreign missionaries and local ministries where leaders are at odds with each other. Ask God to unify them with a single-minded vision for his kingdom.

For the Unsaved

Pray for those who have been raised in the church but who have never put their faith in Jesus and been reconciled to God. Ask that God will open their hearts to him before it's too late.

SEPTEMBER 12

Personal Prayer

Glorify God as the ruler over events both great and small, who knows not only the fate of nations but also the number of hairs on your head (Lk. 12:6-7). Thank God for hearing your prayers. Confess your struggles in prayer to God, and ask for his help and grace in this area (Heb. 4:14-16). Commit yourself to greater discipline in prayer for the needs of others. Ask God to give you wisdom as you pray for specific needs.

For Your Family and Friends

Ask God to strengthen the devotional time of families you know, that it may become a time of sharing, of learning from God's Word, and of prayer for each other.

For the Church

Pray that your church's outreach ministries may be undergirded with a strong foundation of prayer from gifted intercessors in your church, so that God's power will break through the strongholds of Satan in your community.

For the Kingdom

Pray for Christian churches around the world, that they may be known not as "houses of activity" but as "houses of prayer" (Mt. 21:13).

For the Unsaved

Pray today for one unsaved person you know, that God will use you to lead that person "to obey God by what [you] have said and done" (Rom. 15:18).

SEPTEMBER 13

Personal Prayer

Give praise to God as the all-seeing one who knows the smallest detail of the future. Thank God for revealing some things to you about the future. Confess the ease with which you plan for the future without taking into account God's knowledge of what will happen (Jas. 4:13-15). Commit yourself to bringing your plans to him daily, asking his insight and guidance. Ask God to begin preparing you now for the challenges that lie ahead.

For Your Family and Friends

Pray for young people who are concerned about their future—and the elderly who are facing the unknowns of death in their future. Ask God to reassure them of his presence with them always.

For the Church

Pray that the church education program of your church will effectively prepare both adults and children to meet the challenges, work, and possible persecution of the years that lie ahead.

For the Kingdom

Pray for missionaries and teachers in developing countries, that they will have the necessary resources to adequately teach people to read and write and hear the gospel.

For the Unsaved

Pray for the opportunity to talk to someone who has wandered from the truth. Ask God to use you in bringing that person back to Christ (Jas. 5:19-20).

SEPTEMBER 14

Personal Prayer

Glorify God as the Lord who gathers his people from east and west, from north and south, to worship and serve him (Isa. 66:18-21). Thank God for including you as part of this family of varied cultures, races, and languages. Confess any tendency you have to put blinders on, so that you see God as interested only in one people or culture. Commit yourself to studying more about God's work in countries and cultures other than your own. Ask God to give you an opportunity to become involved in that work in some way—by prayer support, financial giving, letter writing, etc.

For Your Family and Friends

Pray for the gift of hospitality among Christian families you know, that they may reach out to people from other cultures or races.

For the Church

Pray that God's Spirit will help your church to move beyond its comfort zone in reaching out to those who are "unfamiliar"—of a different race, creed, or language. Ask God to give you plenty of opportunities to do so.

For the Kingdom

Pray for the day God will "gather all nations and tongues, and they will come and see [his] glory" (66:18). Pray for Christians who have made this vision their life's work.

For the Unsaved

Ask God to show you one person from a different religion whom you can pray for and befriend, perhaps eventually leading him or her to the one true God.

SEPTEMBER 15

Personal Prayer

Praise God as the fair judge and ruler who never lets wealth, appearance, or earthly power influence his decisions. Give thanks for God's constant concern for those in positions of weakness and poverty (Jas. 1:27). Confess those times when your support of the poor has been in word only and not in action (1:22-25). Commit yourself to seeing people as God sees them, not as our society sees them. Ask God to open your eyes to those who are "poor in the eyes of the world to be rich in faith" (Jas. 2:5).

For Your Family and Friends

Pray that the elderly members of these families may be well cared for and visited often, so that they may end their days in comfort and honor rather than loneliness and isolation.

For the Church

Pray for specific individuals and families in your church who may be having a hard time financially. Ask God what you can do to help (Gal. 6:9-10).

For the Kingdom

Ask God to bring relief and comfort to those in India who are treated as less than human because of their social status and circumstances of birth.

For the Unsaved

Pray that unbelievers will be drawn to faith in Christ because of the close-knit, unbiased, and loving fellowship they see in churches in your city or community.

SEPTEMBER 16

Personal Prayer

Praise God as the source of all that you need, in both the spiritual and material realms. Thank God for giving you the ability to produce wealth and to meet basic physical needs. Confess those times when you have thought, "My power and the strength of my hands have produced this wealth for me" (Deut. 8:17-18). Commit yourself to envisioning each day the strength and power of God carrying you along in your work. Ask God to open your eyes to your utter dependence on him.

For Your Family and Friends

Ask God to help parents teach their children to find great enjoyment in giving money, energy, or creativity to the church's ministries. Pray that the parents may set a good example.

For the Church

Pray for those who are materially wealthy in your congregation, that they may be moved "to do good, to be rich in good deeds, and to be generous and willing to share." Thank God for his promise that this leads to a more sure treasure than material wealth (1 Tim. 6:17-19).

For the Kingdom

Intercede for the missionary workers in struggling South American countries, that God may fill them with joy as he supplies even their smallest financial and physical needs with donations and offerings from other churches.

For the Unsaved

Ask God to use even the financial situations of unbelievers to bring them into a dependent trust in his love and promises.

SEPTEMBER 17

Personal Prayer

Give highest praise to God as the all-sufficient one, "El-Shaddai." Thank God for being the strength of your heart and your inheritance forever (Ps. 73:26). Confess to him your reliance on material wealth or possessions to make you feel secure and satisfied. Commit yourself to saying, "Whom have I in heaven but you? And earth has nothing I desire besides you" (73:25). Ask God to help you grasp how completely his love and presence surround you in this day.

For Your Family and Friends

Pray for families who worship amid marital struggles or family tensions. Ask God to meet them in worship with compassion, power, and healing.

For the Church

Ask God to help your church make its worship services a place where unchurched neighbors and guests feel comfortable and welcome, so that they will want to stay and join God's family.

For the Kingdom

Pray for worship services all around the world, that God's Spirit might meet the needs of many hurting and spiritually hungry people who attend.

For the Unsaved

Ask God to reveal to you one person whom you should invite to worship this week or at least invite over for a meal or a cup of coffee.

Prayer Pointer

"It appears that God has so ordered life and the world that our praying is a vital part of his redemptive plan for individuals and the entire universe."
—Maxie Dunnam

SEPTEMBER 18

Personal Prayer

Praise God for the mystery of the Trinity—a model of love, unity, and oneness. Give thanks that God is able to bring a spirit of oneness among you and other believers, "so that with one heart and mouth you may glorify the God and Father of our Lord Jesus Christ" (Rom. 15:5-6). Confess any comments, thoughts, or actions that may have led to division, rather than unity, between you and another Christian. Ask God to make you humble enough to see your own fault in strained relationships and to seek forgiveness and peace.

For Your Family and Friends

Pray that parents may be unified as they teach and discipline their children, creating a God-glorifying harmony in the home.

For the Church

Ask God to put his special protection around the staff and leaders of your church, so that Satan will not be able to bring division through misunderstanding, pride, or self-interest (Phil. 2:1-3).

For the Kingdom

Pray that church leaders from all nations will "agree with each other in the Lord" over potentially divisive issues (Phil. 4:2).

For the Unsaved

Intercede especially for churches in racially mixed neighborhoods, that their witness and harmony may be so powerful that they draw unbelievers of all backgrounds into God's family.

SEPTEMBER 19

Personal Prayer

Praise your Father as the head over the entire family of believers (Eph. 3:14-15). Thank God for the love he lavishes on you and others as he calls you "children of God" (1 Jn. 3:1). Confess those times when you have felt comfortable in your own circle of Christian brothers and sisters and forgotten to reach out to others beyond your own "family." Commit yourself this week to gaining at least one new brother or sister in Christ. Ask God to lead you to a person in your life who is ready to accept the gospel.

For Your Family and Friends

Pray for the believing teenagers you know, that they will be strong enough in their faith to witness to friends who are into drugs or premarital sex or rebellion toward God and their parents.

For the Church

Pray for the midweek outreach efforts of your congregation, that they may result in many neighborhood families coming to know Christ.

For the Kingdom

Ask God to fill all the outreach efforts of his church worldwide with his love, that Christians of all nations will "not love with words or tongue but with actions and in truth" (1 Jn. 3:18).

For the Unsaved

Pray that God will use you this week as the "salt of the earth"—in your actions as well as your words—to bring another person closer to the family of God.

SEPTEMBER 20

Personal Prayer

Praise God as the source of all true wisdom and discernment (Col. 2:3). Thank him for supplying his church with the gifts of wisdom, knowledge, and the ability to distinguish between spirits (1 Cor. 12:8-10). Confess those times when you have failed to discern the cultural influences that try to choke out spiritual growth and fruitfulness. Commit yourself to testing the spirits to see whether they are from God (1 Jn. 4:1). Ask God to make you more aware of the reality of spiritual warfare in your life (Eph. 6:10-12).

For Your Family and Friends

Pray for acquaintances who may be exposed to the occult or New Age philosophy. Ask God to help them discern the falseness of these religions.

For the Church

Pray that God will raise up teachers in your congregation who are gifted in spiritual warfare and who can teach both children and adults how to use all the weapons of the faith against their enemy (6:13-18).

For the Kingdom

Ask God to lift the spiritual blindness from political leaders in your country, that they may make decisions that help create a wholesome and God-honoring society.

For the Unsaved

Pray for your unsaved family members and acquaintances, that God will protect them from false teachers and lead them to the truth.

SEPTEMBER 21

Personal Prayer

Praise God as Jehovah-shammah, "the Lord who is there." Thank God for his immediate and all-encompassing presence in your life (Psalm 139). Confess the times this past week when you have doubted the Lord's presence or acted as though God were not surrounding you with his love and Spirit. Commit yourself to "practicing the presence of God" at all times. Ask him to give you signs of his presence every day this week.

For Your Family and Friends

Intercede for unborn children, that God's hand will be on them even in the womb, protecting and encompassing them with his love.

For the Church

Pray for specific missionaries that you know, that they may experience God's presence strongly as they watch prayers being answered and people brought to the Lord.

For the Kingdom

Ask for God's presence to linger as a fragrance on hospital chaplains as they minister to those facing illness and death.

For the Unsaved

Pray for the large Hindu population in India, that they may turn from dead idols to the living and true God.

Prayer Pointer

"Prayer is the key that opens the door to all that is good in life." —Anonymous

SEPTEMBER 22

Personal Prayer

Give heartfelt praise to God as Jehovah-raah, "the Lord my shepherd." Thank God for leading you into quiet places and restoring your soul as you meet him daily in prayer. Confess those times when you have resisted the discipline and guidance of his shepherd's crook. Commit yourself to becoming so familiar with the Lord's voice that you will follow him without hesitation or fear (Jn. 10:3-5). Ask God to give you a shepherd's heart toward others.

For Your Family and Friends

Intercede for those families whose children are scattered "like sheep without a shepherd," without direction and purpose in their lives.

For the Church

Pray for the elders of your church as they care for those in your fellowship. Ask God to give them sensitivity and a caring heart.

For the Kingdom

Pray that Christian social workers may receive such nurture and care in their church fellowships that they are strengthened to face the difficult task of ministering to a broken world.

For the Unsaved

Pray that the unsaved people you know will come to meet and love their Savior, who wants them to "have life, and have it to the full" (Jn. 10:10).

SEPTEMBER 23

Personal Prayer

Praise the name of Jehovah-jireh, "the Lord will provide." Thank God for having given you everything you need for life and health in this week. Confess to him the times when you have begrudged giving a kind word or encouragement or forgiveness to another person. Commit yourself to reflecting God's generosity and openhanded love to a difficult person in your life. Ask God to give you an extra portion of his Spirit as you strive to reflect his character.

For Your Family and Friends

If there is a specific need in your family that only God can provide, commit this need to him in the faith that he will supply it abundantly (2 Cor. 9:8).

For the Church

Intercede for the churches in your area which work in the inner city and struggle for funds to meet their budgets. Ask God to move the hearts of wealthier congregations to share with them.

For the Kingdom

Praise God for the way in which generous gifts from believers refresh the hearts and spirits of missionaries around the world (9:12-13).

For the Unsaved

Pray for organizations which supply Bibles to motels, hospitals, and foreign countries, that they may not lack funds to bring the Word of life to the unsaved.

SEPTEMBER 24

Personal Prayer

Praise the Lord, the source of all song, and make music to his name. Thank God for his love in the morning and for his faithfulness at night (Ps. 92:1-2). Confess that you sometimes sing by rote. Commit yourself to focusing on what you sing. Ask to feel God's presence through music today.

For Your Family and Friends

As you scan faces in church, ask God to soothe squirming children, sullen teens, and tense adults.

For the Church

Pray that through the music, message, prayers, and sacraments, your congregation will feel one in body and spirit (Eph. 4:3-4) as it gathers to worship.

For the Kingdom

Ask God to extend this spiritual bond so that your church feels one with believers around the world. Consider that believers are called to "one hope . . . one Lord, one faith, one baptism; one God and Father of all, who is over all and through all and in all" (4:4-6).

For the Unsaved

Pray to discern bridges between you or your church and those who are far from God.

Prayer Pointer

"We must try to converse with God in little ways while we do our work; not in memorized prayer, not trying to recite previously formed thoughts. Rather, we should purely and simply reveal our hearts as the words come to us."
—Brother Lawrence

SEPTEMBER 25

Personal Prayer

Praise God, the source of light and Light. Be thankful for the times you've felt the Lord's face shining on you (Ps. 80:3). Confess that you sometimes turn your face from God's. Commit yourself to seeking God's leading. Ask him for confirmation of new directions.

For Your Family and Friends

Petition God to channel peace and clarity through you to family and friends who flounder. Commit yourself to staying close to God, so your life models his leading.

For the Church

Intercede for leaders in your church, so they recognize and know how to carry out Christ's plan for your church. Pledge to express genuine appreciation; God may use your thanks to confirm something for a church leader.

For the Kingdom

Pray that Christian leaders around the world will be led by the Lord alone (Deut. 32:12), despite political, economic, and ethnic ties.

For the Unsaved

Ask God to show you one person who will welcome your spiritual maturity in their life.

Prayer Pointer

"Many pray with their lips for that for which their hearts have no desire."
—Jonathan Edwards

SEPTEMBER 26

Personal Prayer

Praise the Son of Man, who cares about your material needs, your health, and your freedom. Thank him for including you in "proclaim[ing] the year of the Lord's favor" (Lk. 4:18-19). Confess that you give more thought to your family's needs than to the needs of those who have far less. Commit yourself to change. Ask God to open your eyes, heart, time, and finances to a specific person or outreach ministry.

For Your Family and Friends

Pray daily that together with family members or friends you will unite around a ministry cause. Ask for oneness of desire.

For the Church

Implore God to break down unspoken walls of behavior in your church. Resolve to reach out to someone who is overlooked because of his or her differences (Eph. 3:16-19).

For the Kingdom

Pray for courage and faithfulness for North American missionaries who see little results.

For the Unsaved

Ask God to help you care at least as much about unsaved people as you care about the church budget or the order of worship.

SEPTEMBER 27

Personal Prayer

Praise God, your Father and great Teacher. Give thanks for teachers and mentors who helped make your paths straight (Prov. 3:6). Confess that you sometimes focus more on their quirks than their virtues. Commit yourself to noticing the good in those who can teach you more about faith. Ask God how you can best support education in your church.

For Your Family and Friends

Pray that everyone in your church will find something to like in church school, youth group, or adult education. Listen to the experiences of your own children in these settings.

For the Church

Intercede for church educators who try to offer something worthwhile. Ask God to show you new ways to join in.

For the Kingdom

Pray that God's Spirit will lead teachers to discover fresh ways to instruct and disciple new Christians.

For the Unsaved

Claim the Holy Spirit's power to woo family members or friends who say Christianity makes no sense.

Prayer Pointer

"A man's state before God may always be measured by his prayers."—J. C. Ryle

SEPTEMBER 28

Personal Prayer

Praise the God of Abraham, Isaac, and Jacob. Thank him for including you among Abraham's spiritual descendants, for calling you to shine like a star in the firmament of glory (Gen. 22:17). Confess that sometimes your witness is dim. Commit yourself to connecting with and praying for other Christians who want to shine for God. Ask where you should begin.

For Your Family and Friends

Plead with God on behalf of children in your family and those around you. Pray that they will see the spiritual consequences of daily choices—and choose God.

For the Church

Ask God to translate parents' concern for their own children's salvation into passion to make disciples of every nation (Mt. 28:19-20).

For the Kingdom

Lift up missionary families, who often endure long separations from loved ones to share God's good news. Pray that they will enjoy results.

For the Unsaved

Ask God to honor the tentative prayers of those who aren't even sure there is a God—but are beginning to want one.

SEPTEMBER 29

Personal Prayer

Praise God, the Most Holy, worthy of all honor. Give thanks for gatherings where you can join in praise (Ps. 22:22, 25). Confess your reluctance to share such joys outside of Christian circles. Commit yourself to offering glimpses of God's grace to those outside the fellowship. Ask God to show you someone who craves the balm of Gilead (Jer. 46:11).

For Your Family and Friends

Invite God to reveal ways you neglect family or friends as you offer compassion to others. Pray for balance.

For the Church

Ask God to give your congregation joy in being Jesus' hands and feet. Pray for specific ways your church can help others meet their needs for food, income, housing, and transportation.

For the Kingdom

Intercede for North American social workers, who have more cases than time or funds. Ask God to guard them from burnout and cynicism.

For the Unsaved

Ask the Holy Spirit to prompt unbelievers to ask why Christians muck out flooded homes or run food pantries on their behalf.

Prayer Pointer

"The mightier any one is in the Word, the more mighty he will be in prayer."
—William Gurnall

SEPTEMBER 30

Personal Prayer

Praise the Creator, who fills mountain springs, makes grass grow for cattle, and allows people to bring forth food from the earth (Ps. 104:10-14). Thank God for your food and shelter. Confess that all you have belongs to God. Commit to living as a steward, not a consumer. Ask God where to start in renewing your mind-set.

For Your Family and Friends

Ask God to help you find more joy in fresh air, pure water, and bird song than in manufactured goods. Model this among family and friends.

For the Church

Pray for members in your congregation who struggle with huge credit card bills or have trouble meeting their church offering pledge (Mt. 6:21).

For the Kingdom

Ask God to help Christian outreach agencies manage their budgets, so they can pay their employees justly and reach more people.

For the Unsaved

Pray that Christians—by caring more about people than things, by managing money well—will pique interest among non-Christians.

OCTOBER 1

Personal Prayer

Shout Hallelujah! to the Lord God Almighty. Praise God for his power and glory. Thank him for salvation (Rev. 19:1). Confess how rarely in recent days you have meditated on God's wisdom and strength. Commit yourself to thinking more about what you can do for God, rather than what God can do for you. Ask for a renewed sense of awe about God's character, for a greater hunger to know him.

For Your Family and Friends

Pray for family members or friends who hold God at arm's length. Plead for personal peace and joy in Christ, so they will want what you have.

For the Church

Pray that your worship leaders will be sensitive to those with unusual personalities or special needs. Many parts form Christ's body (1 Cor. 12:12-31).

For the Kingdom

Pray that Christians will be willing to examine and change even time-honored forms of worship—if such changes will draw unbelievers to the gospel.

For the Unsaved

Pray that unsaved people who feel empty will find salvation and fulfilling worship.

Prayer Pointer

"Prayer is not conquering God's reluctance, but taking hold of God's willingness."
—Phillips Brooks

OCTOBER 2

Personal Prayer

Praise your Wonderful Counselor, Mighty God, Everlasting Father. Give thanks for the Prince of Peace (Isa. 9:6). Confess how often you'd rather make your own plans than think about what God might be telling you through church leaders. Commit to listening for God through others' words. Ask God to show you whether a specific leader has a word for you.

For Your Family and Friends

Pray for family and friends hurt by church leaders who have misused their influence.

For the Church

Pray for church leaders who must sometimes call for repentance before peace is possible (Josh. 7:1-26).

For the Kingdom

Intercede for leaders throughout the worldwide church. Ask on their behalf for character and integrity, so their actions reflect their convictions.

For the Unsaved

Claim Jesus' power to do your part in gathering in those who are like sheep without a shepherd (Mt. 9:35-38).

OCTOBER 3

Personal Prayer

Praise Jesus, who welcomes the weary. Thank him for lifted burdens (Mt. 11:25-30). Confess that the way you fill your days often ignores Jesus' offer of rest. Commit to enjoying this rest yourself and sharing it with others. Ask God for a specific way you can eliminate something from your schedule in order to create time for resting in the Lord.

For Your Family and Friends

Pray for family and friends who spend much of their time and energy helping others. Ask that they will find their strength in God as they rest quietly in him (Ps. 37:7).

For the Church

Lift up church members who minister in rough schools, rural clinics, nursing homes, and disaster areas.

For the Kingdom

Pray that Christians will multiply God's infinite mercy by befriending people with disabilities, helping released prisoners find work, and sheltering refugees.

For the Unsaved

Pray that you will be more like the Good Samaritan than like the Levite as you meet unsaved people.

Prayer Pointer

"No time is so well spent in every day as that which we spend upon our knees."
—J. C. Ryle

OCTOBER 4

Personal Prayer

Praise God, who calls believers into his kingdom. Thank him for giving you eyes to see and ears to hear the Word (Mt. 13:1-23). Confess that no matter how old you are, you have more to learn. Commit yourself to increasing your knowledge of the faith. Ask God where you should start—personal or group Bible study, church courses, support groups, memorization, singing through a hymnal . . .

For Your Family and Friends

Pray for a willing spirit among family and friends to let God into their lives.

For the Church

Pray that church education leaders will help class members handle tough questions with grace and tolerance.

For the Kingdom

Ask God to use church education programs as springboards to action. Plead for "faith and deeds" churches equal to the test (Jas. 2:1-16).

For the Unsaved

Pray that church school teachers will model the advantages of faith and remind children to pray for unbelievers.

OCTOBER 5

Personal Prayer

Praise God, who "so loved the world that he gave his one and only Son, that whoever believes in him shall not perish but have eternal life" (Jn. 3:16). Thank God for those who led you to Christ. Confess that you are sometimes afraid to introduce others to Christ. Commit yourself to building friendships with people who do not know Jesus. Ask God to help you identify a friend who might be open to conversion.

For Your Family and Friends

Resolve in prayer to talk more among friends and family members about how you as a group can support world missions (Mt. 18:19-20).

For the Church

Lift up missionaries from your church. Write to ask about their special prayer needs.

For the Kingdom

Pray for translators who wrestle with unfamiliar alphabets and languages to spread God's good news to every nation.

For the Unsaved

Ponder in prayer what it will be like when "all the ends of the earth will remember and turn to the LORD" (Ps. 22:27). Pray for the coming of that day.

Prayer Pointer

"Prayer is not merely an occasional impulse to which we respond when we are in trouble: prayer is a life attitude." —WALTER A. MUELLER

OCTOBER 6

Personal Prayer

Praise the Lord, "our dwelling place throughout all generations" (Ps. 90:1). Thank God for the security you've found through faith. Confess ways you've rejected that security this week. Commit yourself to starting each morning satisfied with God's unfailing love (90:14). Ask how you might vary your morning routine to better begin the day with God.

For Your Family and Friends

Pray that God will fill your awareness, so you naturally speak of his care and fellowship in your family and among friends.

For the Church

Pray that Bible studies, households, and cell groups in your congregation will inspire members to deeper bonds and faith-directed action.

For the Kingdom

Lift up advocates for people in wheelchairs or without sight. They need prayers to rewrite laws, redesign buildings, and modify job requirements.

For the Unsaved

Ask God how you or your church could reach out to people with mental disabilities.

OCTOBER 7

Personal Prayer

Praise the Lord your God, who "goes with you; he will never leave you nor forsake you" (Deut. 31:6). Thank God for his presence in your life. Confess times when you think that just a little more money would make you even more content in God's presence (Heb. 13:5). Commit yourself to wanting what you have, rather than scrambling to have what you want. Ask God to simply supply your needs and to give you contentment with his choices.

For Your Family and Friends

Pray that you can teach your children to be generous with their time and money. Involve your friends' children in giving new and used toys to a battered women's shelter.

For the Church

Pray that your congregation will make wise decisions in allocating money for its own ministries, for other Christians, and for unbelievers.

For the Kingdom

Intercede for those who invest money on behalf of Christian agencies.

For the Unsaved

Pray for unbelievers whose poverty erects a wall between them and wealthier Christians.

Prayer Pointer

"Love to pray—feel often during the day the need for prayer, and take trouble to pray." —Mother Teresa

OCTOBER 8

Personal Prayer

Praise God for his sovereignty. Thank him for using ordinary people to prompt effectiveness in the Christian movement. Confess those occasions when you knew God was calling you to take a stand . . . and you didn't. Commit yourself to depending on God's power with renewed faith to act on those opportunities which shape the church of tomorrow (Col. 4:5-6). Ask, "Lord, what can I do to bring about positive change in your church?"

For Your Family and Friends

Pray that your family and friends will receive God's full forgiveness. Pray that they will experience the joy of extending grace to others more freely.

For the Church

Pray that your worship together reflects a celebration of who God is. Pray for the empowerment of all God's children to use their gifts and talents in service of the sovereign Lord.

For the Kingdom

Pray that those engaged in religious cults will recognize that forgiveness is experienced only through Jesus Christ.

For the Unsaved

Ask that unsaved people you know will experience a desire to question the things of our sovereign God.

OCTOBER 9

Personal Prayer

Praise Jesus, the gentle shepherd. Thank him for walking beside you and showing you the way. Ask God to make his presence obvious to you. Confess those times when you failed to recognize the Lord's guidance and protection. Commit yourself to thanking God for his quiet presence.

For Your Family and Friends

Pray that your quiet spirit will touch the hearts of those whom you love and those who are hard to love.

For the Church

Pray that your church leaders will lead your congregation in awe and respect for the gentleness of God.

For the Kingdom

Pray that people in positions of authority will see gentleness as a personal virtue and not a weakness.

For the Unsaved

Pray that the voice of the shepherd will break the hearts of those who desire to be led. Ask that you will be a reflection of his gentle nature (Phil. 4:5).

Prayer Pointer

"The more we receive in silent prayer, the more we can give in our active life."
—Mother Teresa

OCTOBER 10

Personal Prayer

Praise God, for his mercy endures to all generations. Thank him for receiving you without hesitation. Confess thoughts which prevent you from exploring God's mercy. Commit yourself to listening to his still, small voice. Jesus whispers, "Come unto me." Ask God to help you see the many ways he shows you his mercy.

For Your Family and Friends

Pray that God's mercy will be reflected in you in such a way that it becomes a magnetic power drawing your family and friends closer.

For the Church

Pray that God will create tender hearts in his people, the church. Pray for renewed passion to share Christ and his mercy.

For the Kingdom

Pray for Christian psychologists, psychiatrists, and social workers. Ask that they will eagerly share the life-changing, mind-altering power of the Lord Jesus Christ.

For the Unsaved

Pray that the mercy of God will flow through you to unsaved people you know.

OCTOBER 11

Personal Prayer

Praise God, the Creator of the heavens. Thank God for his awesome handiwork, for the beauty reflected in the stars, the moon, the clouds, and the sun. Confess those times when you wondered if God was real and you questioned if he loved you. Commit yourself to praising the Creator of the universe as you see the stars, sun, moon, and clouds. Ask him to provide you peace, knowing that he cares for you.

For Your Family and Friends

Ask God to help you let go of those you worry about. They, too, are in his hands.

For the Church

Intercede for church members who struggle to experience the reality of God. Pray that their faith will be affirmed as they see God in his creation.

For the Kingdom

Pray that those who explore the heavens and earth through science will find not only statistics, but the Creator.

For the Unsaved

Pray that unbelieving people who view the stars tonight will recognize a loving, creative God behind it all.

Prayer Pointer

"God shapes the world by prayer. The more praying there is in the world the better the world will be, the mightier the forces against evil." —E. M. Bounds

OCTOBER 12

Personal Prayer

Praise God, who is the great physician. Thank him for healing broken hearts. Confess those times when you failed to help those who sought to experience the Savior's healing touch. Commit to serving God by serving them. Ask God to reveal names of individuals who suffer from pain, rejection, and spiritual death.

For Your Family and Friends

Pray that God will provide opportunity for you to support the healing of broken hearts through the power of Jesus Christ.

For the Church

Pray for missionaries in foreign countries where modern medicines are not readily available. Ask that God's healing power will become evident in the lives of many.

For the Kingdom

Pray that the physicians and nurses of the world will see human anatomy through the eyes of the great physician.

For the Unsaved

Pray that those experiencing pain will be moved to seek the healing power of the one who suffered pain, rejection, and brokenness for all humankind.

OCTOBER 13

Personal Prayer

Give all your praise to God, for his faithfulness endures forever. In quiet reflection, thank God for his faithful presence during your times of greatest need. With humility, confess your attempts to manage life without him. With a desire to reflect God's faithfulness, commit to recognizing his power. Ask that you will see his faithfulness each day of your life.

For Your Family and Friends

God's faithfulness is communicated through you to others. Pray that you will reflect a sustaining, patient presence with those who observe God in you.

For the Church

Pray that caregivers will be a reminder of the God who empowers them to serve the broken. Pray that the fellowship within the church will be strengthened to reflect God's faithful promises to those he loves.

For the Kingdom

Pray for all marriages. Ask that God will strengthen the commitment between husbands and wives. Pray that our culture will once again embrace the sanctity of matrimony.

For the Unsaved

Pray that those who go to church faith-fully but don't know the faithful Father will hear his voice today and respond in faith.

Prayer Pointer

"To pray is nothing more involved than to open the door, giving Jesus access to our needs and permitting him to exercise his own power in dealing with them."
—O. Hallesby

OCTOBER 14

Personal Prayer

Praise your all-powerful God for conquering sin and death. Thank him for new life in Christ and for saving you from the torment of sin and the agony of eternal death. Confess to God any apathy toward his powerful love in your life. Ask him to develop moment-by-moment awareness of his love for you and a passion to share this love with unbelievers. Commit to praying regularly for unsaved friends, family members, and neighbors. Ask that God will use you to reflect his love, his life, his lordship.

For Your Family and Friends

Pray that the all-powerful God will extend strength to those in your family who call on his name.

For the Church

Pray that your congregation will recognize the importance of faithful stewardship to ministries which unleash God's power.

For the Kingdom

Ask that the effects of sin, death, destruction, and hatred will soon be overcome by the almighty power of the living God.

For the Unsaved

Pray that those who strive for earthly power will come face-to-face with its futility and surrender all to Jesus.

OCTOBER 15

Personal Prayer

Praise God, who is the bread of life. Thank God for the strength he provides you to live each day. Confess those times when you have complained about weakness or yielded to the desire not to press on. Commit yourself to doing those things which nurture spiritual energy. Ask God to reveal to you ways by which he would have you offer "bread" to others.

For Your Family and Friends

Pray that God will provide the energy needed to deal with unexpected circumstances in your family life, remembering that he will sustain you.

For Your Church

Pray that when your congregation gathers around the communion table they will experience the bread as the body of Christ, broken for them.

For the Kingdom

Pray that the farmers across North America will see their fields of wheat and corn as a source of life provided by God.

For the Unsaved

Pray that our cultural spiritual malnutrition will develop into a hunger for the bread of life.

Prayer Pointer

"Set the tone of the day with early morning prayer, and spirituality then tends to prevail and prayer becomes easier." —Ernest B. Gentile

OCTOBER 16

Personal Prayer

Praise God, the Father of all. Thank him for allowing you to call him "Abba"—Daddy. Confess your fear of seeing him as Father. Commit to seeking this attribute of God. Ask God to eliminate any barriers which complicate your ability to experience "Abba" as comforting.

For Your Family and Friends

Let go of the thoughts which hinder you from developing loving relationships with those who seek God.

For Your Church

Pray for sensitivity for those abused by fathers. Pray for ministries to develop which support their healing. Pray that as family units break down the church will be a place where people find family and the reality of God as their Father.

For the Kingdom

Pray for children who are being abused. Pray that their minds and hearts will be protected by the Father, who loves them dearly.

For the Unsaved

Ask God to reveal himself as a loving, welcoming Father to lost and lonely people you know.

OCTOBER 17

Personal Prayer

Praise God, for he is truth. There is no deception in him. Thank God for his revealed redemptive plan. Confess those times when you have doubted the reality of God's righteousness. Commit to faith those things of God which are most difficult for you to accept as his truth. Ask God to help you see his truth revealed to you each day—in nature, in godly relationships, in the renewing of your mind through Christ Jesus.

For Your Family and Friends

Pray that your family and friends will see God's truth in a unique and meaningful way.

For the Church

Pray that your church's efforts to reach others with the gospel of Christ will be securely rooted in the truth of God's Word.

For the Kingdom

Pray that God will reveal the deceit and persuasive powers of false gods and cult leaders.

For the Unsaved

Pray that unbelievers will both respect and accept God's truth.

Prayer Pointer

"Prayer is for the helpless." —O. Hallesby

OCTOBER 18

Personal Prayer

Praise God for his agape love, a liberating power, expressed through selfless acts. Thank God for times when you have experienced his unfailing love for you, his child. Confess those times when you failed to love him. Commit yourself to modeling God's love in all your relationships with others. Ask God to make you sensitive to those occasions when unconditional love can be expressed in your actions.

For Your Family and Friends

Pray that God will give you a vision for what he is accomplishing through the lives of those who are close to you.

For the Church

Thank God for godly mentors who patiently and selflessly teach you how to love and trust God.

For the Kingdom

Ask God to help you view every good and marvelous thing in our culture as his gift.

For the Unsaved

Pray that you will see those who are not yet Christians through the eyes of God—and love them even as he does.

OCTOBER 19

Personal Prayer

Praise God, for he is long-suffering. Thank God for his willingness to suffer for you. Confess those times when you failed to do so, for those times when you lacked patience with God's process. Commit yourself to being willing to suffer for his sake. Ask him for the ability to be long-suffering.

For Your Family and Friends

Ask for a patient, long-suffering attitude with family members or friends who may be especially irritating to you.

For the Church

Pray for missionaries who suffer for the cause of Christ. Pray that they will be encouraged in their task to raise high the cross of Christ.

For the Kingdom

Pray for those change agents who serve to liberate the oppressed.

For the Unsaved

Pray that Christians will be willing to be long-suffering in their service to those who seek Christ.

Prayer Pointer

"Praising God is the secret of having increased blessings in your life." —Don Gossett

OCTOBER 20

Personal Prayer

Praise God for his righteousness. Thank him for the consequences of sin which move you to repentance at the foot of the cross. Confess times of anger when you felt God was not fair. Commit to accepting your circumstances as God's justice at work which shapes his world. Ask God to help you see his righteous acts as acts of love, designed for you.

For Your Family and Friends

Ask God to help you trust his ability to judge those around you. He knows their hearts and their actions.

For the Church

Pray that the caregivers of your church will discern God's justice as it applies to affirming and discipling members of the congregation.

For the Kingdom

Pray for the judges in our courtrooms. Ask that their ability to discern truth will be strong and their wisdom to deal fairly with offenders will be of God.

For the Unsaved

Pray that God's justice will draw sinners to the Savior.

OCTOBER 21

Personal Prayer

Praise God for his comfort. Thank God that he holds you close and calls you his child. Confess those times when you have rejected God's love. Commit yourself to seeking God's comfort through the people in the church and his Word. Ask him to deliver you from your desire to handle your pain alone.

For Your Family and Friends

Pray that you will be a comfort to others within your family structure.

For the Church

Pray that the members of your congregation will reach out in ways which comfort those who are disheartened, discouraged, and depressed.

For the Kingdom

Pray for those who minister to the grieving. Ask that they will enjoy God's richest blessings.

For the Unsaved

Pray that unsaved people will search for and find the comfort that only Jesus can provide.

Prayer Pointer

"Far be it from me that I should sin against the LORD by failing to pray for you."
—1 Samuel 12:23

OCTOBER 22

Personal Prayer

Praise God, whose "every word . . . is flawless." Thank God for being "a shield to those who take refuge in him" (Prov. 30:5). Confess times of not believing or listening to his Word. Commit yourself to hearing God speak to you today. Ask him to truly be your refuge.

For Your Family and Friends

Pray that all those close to you will be especially open to God's Word as it is preached and taught. Ask God to especially use corporate worship times to encourage someone close to you who is struggling right now.

For the Church

As your church gathers for worship this week, pray that the leaders will help the congregation take refuge in God. Ask God's Spirit to lead all worshipers to focus beyond the forms of worship and the details of the service to him.

For the Kingdom

Pray for God's flawless Word to be clearly and practically preached throughout the world. Ask God's Spirit to open hearts so that his kingdom and righteousness may grow.

For the Unsaved

Pray that God will draw unsaved "seekers" to the worship celebrations of his people. Ask God to draw them through his people to himself.

OCTOBER 23

Personal Prayer

Praise the Lord, who is able even to weigh your motives (Prov. 16:2). Thank God for times he has brought conviction to lead you to needed change. Confess any sinful actions, words, plans, or motives the Spirit brings to your attention. Commit to the Lord whatever you are planning to do, asking that he then make your plans succeed (16:3).

For Your Family and Friends

Pray for a pure heart as you lead your children and/or the children of your friends. Ask God to use you as a consistently good example.

For the Church

Pray that the leaders of your church will be motivated by love, faithfulness, and the fear of the Lord rather than pride (16:5-6). Ask God to keep your heart pure toward your leaders and to use you as an encourager for them.

For the Kingdom

Pray for integrity in the lives of Christians in all vocations. Ask God to place thoroughly righteous people in strategic leadership positions in your community and throughout the world.

For the Unsaved

Pray for Christians' consistent love, faithfulness, and fear of the Lord to provide a shining contrast to those caught in deceit. Ask God's Spirit to shine through you to bring someone to his light.

OCTOBER 24

Personal Prayer

Praise the Lord, whose name is a strong tower to which the righteous run and find safety (Prov. 18:10). Thank God for the safety he has brought to your life. Confess any area in which your walk is not consistent with bearing Christ's name. Commit to living all your life under God. Ask him to give you the courage that comes from knowing he cares for you.

For Your Family and Friends

Pray for those in your care to be under the strong tower of God's care. Ask God to assure them of their safety in his strong and tender presence.

For the Church

Pray for the outreach ministries of your local church and the church worldwide. Ask God to cause many unsaved persons to respond to this work, joining the righteous in running to him for safety and life.

For the Kingdom

Pray that the advances in media technology will be used to their best and fullest potential for spreading God's call to safety. Ask God to give his church innovative and visionary understanding of the possibilities for advancing his kingdom.

For the Unsaved

Pray for someone in your neighborhood who is not under the protection of God's name. Ask God for the courage and opportunities to lead that neighbor to your strong tower.

OCTOBER 25

Personal Prayer

Praise God, the source of knowledge (Prov. 1:7). Thank God for the wisdom to apply that knowledge in everyday situations. Confess times of leaning "on your own understanding," not acknowledging him (Prov. 3:5-6). Commit to acknowledging God in all your ways. Ask him to help you trust in him with all your heart.

For Your Family and Friends

Pray that God will open the eyes of children to see his involvement and care in all parts of his creation. Ask God to continually deepen the insights of the adults as well.

For the Church

Pray for your church's education programs. Ask God to lead all to a love for God that grows "more and more in knowledge and depth of insight, so that [they] may be able to discern what is best and may be pure and blameless until the day of Christ, filled with the fruit of righteousness that comes through Jesus Christ—to the glory and praise of God" (Phil. 1:9-11).

For the Kingdom

Pray for teachers and students in all schools to acknowledge God. Ask for special effectiveness for the Christians in these arenas.

For the Unsaved

Pray for neighbors who do not yet "fear the Lord." Ask God to open the eyes of their understanding to know him.

Prayer Pointer

"Through intercessory prayer God does something that would not otherwise be done." —Maxie Dunnam

OCTOBER 26

Personal Prayer

Praise God, the one who ultimately dispenses justice (Prov. 29:26). Thank him for leaders in your country and community who consistently hold up God's just standards. Confess ways in which you have not followed those standards in your own life. Commit to acting justly, loving mercy, and walking humbly with God (Mic. 6:8). Ask God to use you to help bring this way of life to your part of the world.

For Your Family and Friends

Pray for anyone close to you who is apparently not walking humbly with God in the way of justice and mercy. Ask God to establish the work of those who are living rightly with him (Ps. 90:17).

For the Church

Pray for your world missionaries. Ask God to remind them that "fear of man will prove to be a snare, but whoever trusts in the Lord is kept safe" (Prov. 29:25).

For the Kingdom

Pray that world missionaries and their agencies will work to promote God's ways of justice for the societies in which they work. Ask God to give them supernatural effectiveness.

For the Unsaved

Pray also for the individuals in those countries. Ask God to apply the merciful justice of Christ's sacrifice to their lives, leading them to a humble and grateful walk with him.

OCTOBER 27

Personal Prayer

Praise God for being both high above you and intimately within you. Thank God for making you a friend of Jesus as you follow his ways (Jn. 15:14). Confess times of damaging that friendship by acting as if you didn't know Jesus and his ways. Commit to living in loving, obedient partnership with him (15:15). Ask Jesus to increase your appreciation of the gift of his friendship and fellowship.

For Your Family and Friends

Pray for those you love to continually "walk in the ways of good men and keep to the paths of the righteous" (Prov. 2:20). Ask God to give them discretion in choosing friends and associates.

For the Church

Pray for those who administer the caring and fellowship ministries of your local church. Ask God to show you someone who could be served by his care and friendship expressed through you.

For the Kingdom

Pray for Christians in all walks of life to carefully discern the counsel they receive so that they consistently "walk in the ways of good men." Ask God to encourage you through fellow believers to "keep to the paths of the righteous."

For the Unsaved

Pray for acquaintances who apparently are neither "good" nor "righteous." Ask God to convict them by his Spirit (Jn. 16:8-11) so that they turn to him.

OCTOBER 28

Personal Prayer

Praise the sovereign one who works out everything for his own ends (Prov. 16:4). Thank God for determining your steps (16:9). Confess any area where you may be doubting that his leading is best. "Commit to the LORD whatever you [are planning to] do," knowing that then "your plans will succeed" (16:3). Ask the Lord to alter any plans that are not fully in line with his best.

For Your Family and Friends

Pray for anyone close who seems more interested in the riches of this world than those of God. Ask God to help all to remember that it is far "better to get wisdom than gold, to choose understanding rather than silver" (16:16).

For the Church

Pray for Christians to give cheerfully and generously of this world's resources for leading many to the riches of God. Ask God to give great discernment to those managing ministry resources.

For the Kingdom

Pray for relief from poverty for one of the nations in the news. Ask God to bless the work of Christian relief agencies and others seeking to help.

For the Unsaved

Pray that Christians' generosity will shine beautifully in the darkness of our materialistic culture. Ask God to draw many through this light to exchange their trinkets for his true treasure.

OCTOBER 29

Personal Prayer

Praise God for his faithfulness (2 Cor. 1:18). Give thanks that "no matter how many promises God has made, they are 'Yes' in Christ" (1:20). Confess any reluctance to trust God. Commit to consciously remembering that God has "anointed us, set his seal of ownership on us, and put his Spirit in our hearts as a deposit, guaranteeing what is to come" (1:21-22). Ask him to lead you in celebrating this faithfulness in worship.

For Your Family and Friends

Pray for a thankful, trusting spirit for your household. Ask God to increase the joy of fellow worshipers through your attitude.

For the Church

Pray for faithfulness to God by those who explain his Word. Ask God to clearly speak through them in a resounding affirmation of his "'Yes' in Christ" (1:18-20).

For the Kingdom

Pray for all who listen to God's Word explained. Ask God's Spirit to point out specific applications to people in all walks of life, showing them how to seek his kingdom and righteousness in their part of his world.

For the Unsaved

Pray for the actions and attitudes of God's people as they go out into your community to impact the unsaved. Ask God to use the faithfulness of his people to draw many to himself.

OCTOBER 30

Personal Prayer

Praise "the God and Father of the Lord Jesus, who is to be praised forever" (2 Cor. 11:31). Thank him for giving you spiritual leaders, past and present, who have led you in walking with God. Confess times of veering away on ungodly sidetracks. Commit yourself to following leaders who truly follow Christ, and ask God to use you as a godly leader for someone else.

For Your Family and Friends

Pray by name for those called to be the spiritual leaders in the households of your family and friends. Ask God's Spirit to prompt them to the diligence such a great responsibility requires.

For the Church

Pray for the leaders of your denomination and local church ministries. Ask God to give them vision, compassion for those they lead, and his strength to sustain them as they "face daily the pressure of [their] concern" for those under their care (11:28-29).

For the Kingdom

Pray for believers in all walks of life to be God-honoring leaders in their work environments. Ask God to strengthen them as they often must lead against the flow of cultural currents.

For the Unsaved

Pray for an unsaved person in your neighborhood. Ask God for the privilege of being a godly influence in that person's life, leading him or her to follow Christ.

OCTOBER 31

Personal Prayer

Praise Jesus Christ, the Lord, the image of God (2 Cor. 4:4-5). Thank God for making "his light shine in our hearts to give us the light of the knowledge of the glory of God in the face of Christ" (4:6). Confess times of disinterest in knowing God fully. Commit yourself to thinking daily about him and his glory. Ask God to make his light shine more fully in your heart.

For Your Family and Friends

Pray for God to shine through you to your family and friends, even though they know you well enough to see your weaknesses. Thank God that this shows even more clearly that the power is from him rather than you (4:7).

For the Church

Pray for God's light to shine in your community through your church's members. Ask God to help people focus on the glory of his light rather than on the failings of his light-bearers.

For the Kingdom

Pray for those working to begin new churches. Ask God to bring his light to more and more areas through these new communities of believers.

For the Unsaved

Pray for many unsaved people to be reached through small group Bible studies and Sunday school. Ask God to use you and other believers, in spite of frailties, to bring his light to many.

NOVEMBER 1

Personal Prayer

Praise the meek and gentle Christ, who has power to demolish strongholds (2 Cor. 10:1, 4). Thank God for his truth and power, which are so different from the world's. Confess times of placing ultimate reliance in mere human resources. Commit to putting your confidence and pride in the Lord (10:17). Ask God to guide you to live in such a way that you receive his commendation, no matter what the world says (10:18).

For Your Family and Friends

Pray for your households to be founded upon the principles of God rather than the mere "wisdom" of this world. Ask God to guide and protect your home with his truth.

For the Church

Pray for those in the church's education ministries. Ask God to give them the wisdom and courage to lead God's people to "demolish arguments and every pretension that sets itself up against the knowledge of God . . . [taking] captive every thought to make it obedient to Christ" (10:5).

For the Kingdom

Pray for God's people in all walks of life to "aim for perfection" (2 Cor. 13:11). Ask God to use their clear thinking to extend his kingdom and righteousness.

For the Unsaved

Pray by name for unsaved friends and neighbors. Ask God to break through ungodly thinking and replace it with the Truth who can set them free.

NOVEMBER 2

Personal Prayer

Praise the sovereign God who opens doors for the gospel of Christ (2 Cor. 2:12). Thank God for leading you "in triumphal procession in Christ" and using you to spread "the fragrance of the knowledge of him" (2:14). Confess any lack of desire to be part of this procession. Commit to joining this great procession, and ask God to use you to bring "the knowledge of him" to your areas of influence.

For Your Family and Friends

Pray for each member of your household to be filled with God's missionary Spirit. Ask him to show your household how to be most effectively involved in mission work.

For the Church

Pray that God's missionaries "not peddle the word of God for a profit" but rather "speak before God with sincerity, like men sent from God" (2:17). Ask God to honor such selflessness.

For the Kingdom

Pray for the freedom to proclaim God's Word fully and openly in all countries. Ask for protection and great fruitfulness for missionaries who have left homelands to bring God's promise to the world.

For the Unsaved

Pray for those for whom "the aroma of Christ" in the "triumphal procession" is "the smell of death," asking God to work his grace into their hearts to change it to "the fragrance of life" (2:14-17).

NOVEMBER 3

Personal Prayer

Praise "the God and Father of our Lord Jesus Christ, the Father of compassion and the God of all comfort" (2 Cor. 1:3). Thank God for coming to you with his compassion and comfort in your times of need. Confess insensitivity toward others who need you to be a channel of God's compassion and comfort. Commit to an openhearted lifestyle. Ask God to love someone through you this week.

For Your Friends and Family

Pray that the love among those close to you be that which comes from God. We often tend to be more compassionate to others than to those with whom we live on a daily basis, so ask especially for compassion toward those closest to you.

For the Church

Pray for the caregiving and fellowship ministries of your church. Ask God to provide visionary deacons to lead you and your local congregation in showing the love of Christ.

For the Kingdom

Pray for Christian relief agencies around the world. Ask God to give his supernatural strength to workers in the midst of intense need.

For the Unsaved

Pray for the unsaved to be warmed and opened by the compassion and comfort brought by God's people. Ask that they be moved to accept God's central compassion and comfort in the person of Christ Jesus.

NOVEMBER 4

Personal Prayer

Praise God, who "is able to make all grace abound to you, so that in all things at all times, having all that you need, you will abound in every good work" (2 Cor. 9:8). Thank God for his abundant grace to you. Confess times of hoarding God's resources, as if his loving supply for you were not continuous. Commit to being "generous on every occasion," asking that such "generosity will result in thanksgiving to God" (9:11).

For Your Family and Friends

Pray for a generous spirit to be prominent and pervasive. Ask God to bring the joy of giving to even very young children.

For the Church

Praise God for believers who have "rich generosity," at times giving even beyond their normal ability in self-sacrificing love. Thank him especially for those who give themselves first to the Lord and then to each other, and ask that such generosity be multiplied in many others (2 Cor. 8:1-5).

For the Kingdom

Pray for the great array of Christian ministries seeking to meet needs around the world. Ask God to richly supply the resources needed.

For the Unsaved

Pray that Christians' generous "obedience that accompanies [their] confession of the gospel of Christ," will result in people praising God (2 Cor. 9:13). Ask God to draw the unsaved to himself through this joyful generosity.

NOVEMBER 5

Personal Prayer

Praise God for his Word that is so available for meaningful worship. Give thanks for the power to minister in God's name (Lk. 9:1-3). Confess those times when you neglect God's Word or fail to spend daily time with him (Lk. 18:1). Commit yourself to teaching, fellowship, and prayer (Acts 2:42). Ask God to bless you and to "enlarge [your] territory" with his power, presence, and protection (1 Chron. 4:10).

For Your Family and Friends

Ask God to use his Word in your life to teach, rebuke, correct, and train others in your family (2 Tim. 3:16).

For the Church

Pray that God will increase your faith through corporate worship. Ask that your pastor not compromise God's Word, even though methods of communicating that Word may change.

For the Kingdom

Ask God to enlarge the ministry and influence of Bible societies which make his Word available in lands around the world.

For the Unsaved

Pray that your knowledge of the Word will be used in love as you befriend an unbeliever.

Prayer Pointer

"Prayer is striking the winning blow; service is gathering up the results. You can do more than pray after you have prayed, but you cannot do more than pray until you have prayed." —S. D. Gordon

NOVEMBER 6

Personal Prayer

Praise God that he is coming with the clouds and every eye shall see him (Rev. 1:7). Give thanks that you have a personal relationship with God and will be with him for all eternity (1 Cor. 15:51-52). Confess your clinging to a sinful deed or habit that needs to be overcome. Commit yourself to being on guard and standing firm in your faith (Eph. 6:13-18). Ask God to hold that vision of glory before you, restraining you from strong attachment to earthly possessions.

For Your Family and Friends

Pray that those you love will recognize God's power and glory in his coming again, but also in their lives each day.

For the Church

Ask that the leaders of your church will be faithful examples of God's power, never being ashamed to testify of our Lord (2 Tim. 1:7-12).

For the Kingdom

Pray for every Christian to know and believe that godliness with contentment is great gain (1 Tim. 6:6).

For the Unsaved

Ask that you never be ashamed of the gospel of Jesus Christ for it is the power of God for salvation (Rom. 1:16). Share that salvation today with a non-Christian.

Prayer Pointer

"If I commit myself for the day to the Lord Jesus, then I may rest assured that it is his eternal, almighty power which has taken me under its protection and which will accomplish everything for me." —Andrew Murray

NOVEMBER 7

Personal Prayer

Praise God that he is the Chief Shepherd, preparing for you the crown of glory that will not fade (1 Pet. 5:4). Thank him for leading you like a shepherd to well-watered gardens. Confess those times you stray like a lost sheep and forget God's commands (Ps. 119:176). Commit your life to doing what is pleasing to God (Heb. 13:20-21). Ask him to help you recognize false prophets who come to you in sheep's clothing, but inwardly are ferocious wolves (Mt. 7:15).

For Your Family and Friends

Many have family members who are like sheep without a shepherd (Mt. 9:36). Pray that God will use you as a shepherd in some way today.

For the Church

Pray that your church will reach out in love and not judgment to members who have strayed. Ask that they again may find the security of the good shepherd (John 10).

For the Kingdom

Jim Elliott wrote: "He is no fool who gives what he cannot keep to gain what he cannot lose." Pray that you will be a sharing and giving person in God's kingdom.

For the Unsaved

Pray that by "giving something that you cannot keep" to one in need today, another may receive the gift of salvation.

NOVEMBER 8

Personal Prayer

Praise God for his command to serve him faithfully with all your heart, considering what great things he has done for you (1 Sam. 12:24). Thank God for the greatest of all gifts, salvation in Jesus Christ (Jn. 3:16). Confess your lack of faith as you attempt to flee from God in the midst of trying circumstances (1 Kings 19). Commit yourself to growing in the knowledge and grace of God, giving him the glory (2 Pet. 3:18). Ask God to show you daily how your faith is a Fantastic Adventure In Trusting Him.

For Your Family and Friends

Pray for God to increase your faith as well as the faith of all those close to you, reflecting how God takes care of the grass and flowers, and even more so of you (Mt. 6:26-30).

For the Church

Pray that every teacher in your church will be a living example of great faith because of something God has done or is doing in his or her life right now (Heb. 11:1).

For the Kingdom

Pray that joy and gladness may be found throughout God's kingdom, with thanksgiving and songs of gladness for God's faithfulness to all generations (Isa. 51:11).

For the Unsaved

Pray that the joy and gladness of an active faith in Christians throughout the world will speak to the hearts of the unsaved, so their desire will be to serve the Lord (Jas. 2:14, 17).

NOVEMBER 9

Personal Prayer

Praise God that he speaks in ways that even the lonely, anguished, and defeated can understand (2 Cor. 1:3-4). Give thanks that all things are possible in God (Mt. 19:26). Confess the many times you are tempted to work things out yourself, or are enmeshed in self-pity (Rom. 8:28). Commit to God all who are defeated and lonely. Ask God to help you remember that all you do is to be done in the name of Jesus, giving thanks and glory to him (Col. 3:17).

For Your Family and Friends

Trust God to instill in you the desire to share your physical and spiritual possessions with family members or friends in need (1 Jn. 3:17; Heb. 13:15-16).

For the Church

Pray that God will give your church a heart for reaching the nations of the world for Christ, through encouragement of missionaries, through giving, and through prayers.

For the Kingdom

Pray specifically for the distribution of Bibles throughout the world and for the financial means to continue this important work.

For the Unsaved

Ask God to use these Bibles as a means of salvation for many who receive them as they are given in the name of Jesus with much prayer.

NOVEMBER 10

Personal Prayer

Praise God for his teaching to be of good cheer even in a world of tribulation (Jn. 16:33). Thank God for being your shelter in times of trouble (Ps. 91:1-2). Confess personal burdens that you haven't committed to him and which rob you of that "good cheer" (2 Cor. 5:4). Commit yourself to trusting Christ in every situation (1 Cor. 10:13). Ask God to reveal himself in a special way to his children who feel distant from him today.

For Your Family and Friends

Intercede for any of your family members or friends who are suffering intensely today. Ask God not to withhold his mercy. Pray that his love and truth will protect them (Ps. 40:11).

For the Church

Pray that God will use you and other compassionate people in your church to help those with special needs today.

For the Kingdom

There are so many sheep in God's kingdom. Pray for God to gather them in by using his people everywhere to feed, care for, and love them (Jn. 21:15-17).

For the Unsaved

Ask God to give you sensitivity to any unsaved person who asks you about our troubled world. Pray for eyes to see that as an opportunity to speak of the hope you have in Jesus (1 Tim. 6:17-19).

Prayer Pointer

"Praying for people will bring you to love them. Loving them will lead you to serve them. Serving them will be the open door through which God can move in to save, heal, and make whole."—Maxie Dunnam

NOVEMBER 11

Personal Prayer

Praise God whose kingdom is not a matter of eating and drinking but of righteousness, peace, and joy in the Holy Spirit (Rom. 14:17). Thank God for his kindness and love in Jesus, who saved you by the shedding of his own blood (Titus 3:4-7). Confess those times of subtle boasting of how much you do for the Lord and his church (2 Cor. 11:21-30). Commit yourself to quietly helping another person through prayer, encouragement, or deed without self-recognition. Ask God to keep you from pride (Rom. 11:20).

For Your Family and Friends

Pray for your family and friends to spend quality time together, building firm foundations in their faith (1 Cor. 3:8-17).

For the Church

Ask that your church will spend time encouraging and equipping members, warning those who are idle, helping the weak—being the best possible stewards of time as well as money (1 Thess. 5:11-21).

For the Kingdom

Pray that impoverished Christians all over the world will continue to teach the "financially fit" that happiness and eternal joy are found in Jesus, not in "things."

For the Unsaved

Pray that God will give you an opportunity (and that you will use it) to share with one who is "rich" in this world but "poor" in spirit (Mt. 5:3).

NOVEMBER 12

Personal Prayer

Praise your great, mighty, and awesome covenant-keeping God (Neh. 9:32). Thank God for strengthening those whose hearts are fully committed to him (2 Chron. 16:9). Confess those times when you depend on your own strength rather than God's (Eccl. 5:7). Commit yourself to spending time daily reflecting on God's awe, his faithfulness, and might (Ps. 89:6-8). Ask God's forgiveness for neglecting him when hardships arise.

For Your Family and Friends

Pray that God will reassure your family that he does care for them and will restore their fortunes even as the great day of the Lord draws near (Zeph. 2:3, 7).

For the Church

Pray that your congregation will reflect on the Lord's righteousness and justice in worship this week (Zeph. 3:5).

For the Kingdom

Pray that God's kingdom will grow as oppressed people recognize God's awesome majesty and come to him in faith.

For the Unsaved

Pray for God to use you today to lead an oppressed unbeliever to recognize God's awesome majesty.

Prayer Pointer

"Worship is intended to introduce God's kingdom power throughout the church and extend that power through the church." —Jack Hayford

NOVEMBER 13

Personal Prayer

Praise God that your sighing is not hidden from him (Ps. 38:9). Give thanks that you can cast all your care on him because he cares for you (1 Pet. 5:7). Confess to God the many times you worry, are fearful, or trust in something other than God (Ps. 37:5-6). Commit yourself to daily food from God's Word and time with him in prayer. Ask God for victorious faith that overcomes the world (1 Jn. 5:4).

For Your Family and Friends

Ask that your family will be reminded of God's goodness and faithfulness through your example of giving him all the glory in every situation.

For the Church

Pray that your church will be living proof of the fact that God fulfills the desires of those who fear him (Ps. 145:19).

For the Kingdom

Pray that you will be a consistent example of God's love today and always—and thereby help to advance God's kingdom on earth.

For the Unsaved

In whatever difficult circumstances you find yourself, pray for God to use you as a springboard for the salvation of an unbeliever.

NOVEMBER 14

Personal Prayer

Praise God that you are his temple (1 Cor. 3:16). Thank God for the work he's given you to build up Christ's body, the church (Eph. 4:16). Confess those times you do not honor God with your body, as he has purchased you with the price of his blood (1 Cor. 6:19-20). Commit yourself to Jesus' cleansing of your total being (Jn. 13:8-10). Ask God to reveal to you daily the mystery of his glorious riches (Col. 1:26-27).

For Your Family and Friends

Pray that your family and friends will not dwell on outward beauty but on the unfading beauty of the inner self, a gentle and quiet spirit (1 Pet. 3:3-4).

For the Church

Pray that your church's outreach ministry to the needy in your community will be a beautiful example of Christian servanthood.

For the Kingdom

Pray for many more full-time kingdom workers all over the world and for Christians to respond to God's call saying, "Here am I, send (use) me" (Isa. 6:8).

For the Unsaved

Ask that your love, which comes from a pure heart, good conscience, and sincere faith, will be instrumental in leading unsaved friends to Christ (1 Tim. 1:5).

Prayer Pointer

"Prayer enlarges the heart until it is capable of containing God's gift of himself. Ask and seek, and your heart will grow big enough to receive him and keep him as your own." —Mother Teresa

NOVEMBER 15

Personal Prayer

Praise God for choosing the foolish things of the world to shame the wise and the weak things to shame the strong (1 Cor. 1:27). Thank God that your salvation does not depend on your wisdom but on his grace alone (Eph. 2:8-9). Confess your self-sufficiency (Lk. 16:11-13). Commit yourself to doing what the Lord requires of youto act justly, love mercy, and walk humbly with your God (Mic. 6:8). Ask God to show you clearly the depth of the riches of wisdom and knowledge of God (Rom. 11:33).

For Your Family and Friends

Pray for family members who live outside the family of God. Ask that they will come to know the wisdom of God found only in Christ Jesus.

For the Church

Pray that your church leaders will show God's wisdom by their godly lives and deeds done in the humility that comes from wisdom (Jas. 3:13).

For the Kingdom

Pray for godly wisdom to be given in great abundance to leaders of worldwide mission agencies. Pray that they will be kept from making wrong choices as they seek to advance God's kingdom throughout the earth.

For the Unsaved

Ask that God will clearly show you the place he would have you serve so that you might be an effective witness to the unsaved (Eph. 5:1).

NOVEMBER 16

Personal Prayer

Praise Jesus, who is the gate of salvation (Jn. 10:7-10). Thank him for bringing you through that gate and for the security you find inside. Confess those times when you seek security in something other than Jesus. Commit yourself to being a doorkeeper in the house of God rather than dwelling in the tents of wickedness (Ps. 84:10). Ask God to use you to attract those outside of Christ to enter into a saving relationship with him.

For Your Family and Friends

Pray that those close to you will have thankful hearts in every situation.

For the Church

Pray that your church will march triumphantly against the hosts of Satan, with the assurance that the gates of hell cannot prevail against God's church (Mt. 16:18).

For the Kingdom

Pray for the protection of God's people throughout the world. Ask that they will strongly resist Satan's attacks (Jas. 4:7).

For the Unsaved

Pray that you will open your doors of love to those outside of Christ, that some may yet gain entrance to the door of heaven.

Prayer Pointer

"Do not be anxious about anything, but in everything, by prayer and petition, with thanksgiving, present your requests to God. And the peace of God, which transcends all understanding, will guard your hearts and your minds in Christ Jesus." —PHILIPPIANS 4:6-7

NOVEMBER 17

Personal Prayer

Praise God for his glorious grace freely given in his Son, Jesus Christ (Eph. 1:6). Thank him for an outpouring of the Spirit of the Lord (2 Cor. 3:17). Confess those times when the exercise of your freedom has become a stumbling block to the weak (1 Cor. 8:9). Commit yourself to walking in the freedom of God's Word (Ps. 119:45). Ask God to make you a slave of righteousness (Rom. 6:18).

For Your Family and Friends

Pray that the Lord will set your family and friends free from painful memories.

For the Church

Pray for the caregivers of your church to be especially helpful to believers who are in unhappy marriages with unbelievers (1 Cor. 7:14).

For the Kingdom

Praise God that believers are all baptized by the Spirit into one body—whether Jew or Greek, slave or free—and are all given the same Spirit (1 Cor. 12:13).

For the Unsaved

Pray for people you know who are still slaves to sin. Ask God to show them through you that he has not deserted them but is waiting patiently for salvation to come to their house (Acts 16:29-32).

NOVEMBER 18

Personal Prayer

Praise God for the good gifts he gives to those who ask him (Mt. 7:11). Give thanks, even in the midst of pain all around, that God's gifts are good. Confess your lack of quality time spent with God in prayer (Rom. 8:26). Commit yourself to modeling Jesus' example of praying in solitary places (Mk. 1:35). Ask God to give you a real devotion to prayer—being watchful and thankful, making the most of every opportunity (Col. 4:2-5).

For Your Family and Friends

Pray for family members and friends who are facing the imminent death of a loved one. Ask that they will sense the real comfort that prayer offers in such times.

For the Church

Pray that your church members will generously give of their time and money so that pleas for more will not be necessary (2 Cor. 9:6-7).

For the Kingdom

Pray that God will instill in Christians around the world the desire to pray faithfully and fervently (Prov. 15:8, 29).

For the Unsaved

Ask God to use emergency or crisis situations in the lives of unsaved people to bring them to the foot of the cross. Pray for eyes to see how you can help in such situations.

Prayer Pointer

"One of the most common weaknesses of our prayer lives is the vagueness of our focus. . . . Petition saves us from that. It forces us to be specific, to be precise, to clarify our wants and desires." —Maxie Dunnam

NOVEMBER 19

Personal Prayer

Praise God, the one who is your "refuge" and your "fortress" (Ps. 91:2). Thank him for taking care of you in every storm of life. Confess times when you've sought refuge in some thing or someone other than God. Commit yourself to placing all your trust in this powerful and loving God. Ask God to protect and defend you against Satan's schemes.

For Your Family and Friends

Ask God to make your home a spiritual refuge from the temptations of this world. Pray that your children will find strength, peace, and security there. Pray for harmony among the members of your family.

For the Church

Pray for the worship of your congregation. Intercede for all who lead and for all who participate. Ask God to keep your church's worship focused solely on him.

For the Kingdom

Ask God to break down human barriers and fortresses designed to shut out the gospel throughout the world. Pray for believers who live and worship under the oppression of godless governments. Pray that God will be their refuge.

For the Unsaved

Ask God to open your eyes to the needs of unbelieving people around you. Pray for opportunities to befriend them and to share your faith.

NOVEMBER 20

Personal Prayer

Praise God, the one who is your dwelling place (Ps. 90:1). Thank him for giving you a wonderful inheritance in Jesus Christ, "an inheritance that can never perish, spoil, or fade" (1 Pet. 1:4). Confess moments during the past day or week when you've looked for other "dwelling places." Commit yourself to living under the authority and love of your heavenly Father. Ask God to show you today why his "dwelling place" is the best.

For Your Family and Friends

If you come from a line of believers, give thanks to God for being the dwelling place of generations past. Pray for his grace to be shown to generations yet to come.

For the Church

Intercede for the families of your pastor(s), elders, and deacons. Ask that God will be their dwelling place, too. Pray that these church leaders will find great joy both at home and in their work in your congregation.

For the Kingdom

Pray that God will gather together all those throughout the world who are searching for him as their dwelling place, and will bring them into the light of his marvelous, redeeming grace. Ask God to use you in that great gathering worldwide.

For the Unsaved

Pray that you will be enabled to show to an unbeliever by your word and deed why it is that you trust God as your dwelling place.

NOVEMBER 21

Personal Prayer

Praise God, the one who is your "light" and your "salvation" (Ps. 27:1). Thank him for shining his saving light in your darkness. Confess times when you've preferred to live in the darkness of sinful actions and habits rather than in the light of Jesus. Commit yourself anew to living in his light. Ask God to surround you every day this week with his light and salvation.

For Your Family and Friends

Pray for opportunities to spread God's light in the lives of any family member or friend who does not know Jesus as Savior and Lord. Ask God to touch their lives with the gospel.

For the Church

Intercede for the outreach ministries of your church and denomination. Pray that their financial needs will be met. Ask that they will clearly show forth the light of the good news through their ministries.

For the Kingdom

Pray for Christian ministries which bring healing light into some of our society's darkest corners. Pray for those who work with the homeless, with substance abusers, with the poor, with persons in mental institutions, and others. Ask that the love of Jesus will soothe every hurting heart.

For the Unsaved

Pray by name for someone you know who has not yet committed his or her life to Christ. Ask God to reveal how you can be a spiritual help to that person.

NOVEMBER 22

Personal Prayer

Praise God for all his mighty works (Ps. 46:8-10), for his power, his majesty, his magnificent splendor over all the earth. Thank God for this psalm's very clear and uplifting picture of God's grandeur. Confess that you sometimes live as if God were small, powerless, and expendable. Commit yourself to serving this grand and glorious God with humility and reverence. Ask God to reveal something of his splendor in your life this week.

For Your Family and Friends

Pray that believers among your family and friends will have this same view of God. Pray that their lives will reflect his majesty.

For the Church

Intercede for the educational ministry of your church. Pray for those who teach and for those who are learners. Ask God to raise up dedicated and gifted teachers in your congregation. Thank him for quality curriculum materials.

For the Kingdom

Pray for evangelical seminaries and Bible schools in the U.S. and Canada which are training pastors, evangelists, and teachers for the work of ministry. Ask God to meet their financial needs. Pray for more young Christians to study and train for pastoral ministry.

For the Unsaved

Pray that "the works of the Lord" might be so evident as to draw unbelievers to saving faith in Jesus Christ. Ask for spiritual blinders to be removed.

NOVEMBER 23

Personal Prayer

Praise God, the one who is never far away from his children. Thank him for being close to you when you feel brokenhearted or crushed in spirit (Ps. 34:18). Confess your own unwillingness to have a God so near. Commit yourself to drawing near to God in daily prayer and fellowship (Jas. 4:8). Ask him to bless you by his presence throughout your life.

For Your Family and Friends

Pray that believing family members and friends also will draw near to God. Uphold them in their personal devotional lives.

For the Church

Intercede for the great worldwide mission effort of the church. Ask God to raise up more workers to enter the harvest around the world. Pray specifically for missionaries whom you know or support financially.

For the Kingdom

Thank God for the work of chaplains who minister in God's name in prisons, hospitals, schools, and the armed forces throughout North America. Ask God to bless their work and witness.

For the Unsaved

Ask God to enable an unsaved friend you know to reach out to him in faith. Thank God for the promise that those who seek him with a believing heart will find him (Acts 17:27).

Prayer Pointer

"God does nothing on earth save in answer to believing prayer." —John Wesley

NOVEMBER 24

Personal Prayer

Praise God, the one who strengthens and helps you (Isa. 41:10). Give thanks for God's promise to be with you when you "pass through the rivers" or "walk through the fire" (Isa. 43:2). Confess those times when you've doubted God's loving presence and care. Commit yourself to trusting in God to protect and defend you. Ask him to increase your faith.

For Your Family and Friends

Pray for the marriages of your family and friends. Intercede especially for any who are pursuing divorce. Pray that those marriages will be healed.

For the Church

Ask God to make your congregation a warm and loving church to all. Pray for a spirit of concern and humility as you reach out to the needs of other members and beyond.

For the Kingdom

Pray for the political leaders of your country. Ask that they will be men and women of integrity and honor. Pray that their primary allegiance will be to God alone.

For the Unsaved

Ask God to encourage those who are seeking. Pray that they soon will come to God in repentance and faith.

Prayer Pointer

"We are now in the beginning stages of the greatest movement of prayer in living memory." —C. Peter Wagner

NOVEMBER 25

Personal Prayer

Praise God, the one who keeps you in perfect peace (Isa. 26:3). Give thanks for peace which is far beyond your understanding (Phil. 4:7). Confess that you sometimes look to the world to bring you peace rather than to God. Commit yourself to living in peace with others (1 Thess. 5:13). Ask God to give you a peaceable spirit.

For Your Family and Friends

Pray for the peace of God to spread throughout your home. Ask him to bring about peaceful resolution to any ongoing strife in your family.

For the Church

Ask that God's peace will reassure those who tithe regularly and give sacrificially in your church. Pray that they will not suffer due to their commitment to financial stewardship.

For the Kingdom

Pray for peace in various denominations of Christ's church where Satan is causing division. Pray for your own denomination. Ask for repentance and renewed commitment to follow Jesus.

For the Unsaved

Jesus promises to give his peace to those who believe in faith (Jn. 14:27). Pray for one unsaved person you know to receive Jesus' precious peace.

NOVEMBER 26

Personal Prayer

Give praise to God who is the ruler of all things (1 Chron. 29:12). Thank him for his mighty and powerful acts. Confess times when you've questioned God's power by trusting in your own strength. Commit yourself to exalting God in everything you do this week. Ask him to give you strength to live for him.

For Your Family and Friends

Uphold members of your family who are in special need, who have suffered loss of some kind, or who need encouragement.

For the Church

Pray for the children who worship regularly in your congregation. Ask that they will sense the important role they play in the life of your church.

For the Kingdom

Give thanks to God for the spread of the gospel throughout the world. Pray that worshiping churches will be pleasing to him.

For the Unsaved

Pray by name for an unsaved friend, relative, or coworker. Ask God to open this person's spiritual eyes to the wonder of new life in Christ.

Prayer Pointer

"Prayer is obedience! God's command and promise is our motive for prayer."
—John Calvin

NOVEMBER 27

Personal Prayer

Praise the infinite God who has no beginning and no end. Thank God that with him all things are possible (Lk. 1:37). Confess any lack of faith concerning God's ways and works. Commit yourself anew to living obediently before God. Ask him to keep your eyes focused on Jesus.

For Your Family and Friends

Pray today for any who are newly married among your family or friends. Ask that their love will grow strong and that they will base their relationship on the solid rock of Christ.

For the Church

Ask God to give joy to the elders and deacons of your church. Pray that the many meetings they attend and the extra responsibility they carry will not be burdensome to them.

For the Kingdom

Pray for justice and righteousness to come to the nations of this world which seek to block the work of the Lord (Ps. 2:1-2). Ask that their rulers will bow to Jesus and begin to serve him (2:10-11; Isa. 60:3).

For the Unsaved

Pray for the work of godly evangelists around the world who fearlessly preach the gospel to lost people. Ask that their labors be rewarded.

NOVEMBER 28

Personal Prayer

Praise God as the one whose arm is "not too short to save, nor his ear too dull to hear" (Isa. 59:1). Thank God for the promise to hear you when you come to him in prayer. Confess any sin which may result in his not hearing your prayers (59:2). If you are struggling in this area, commit yourself to regular, daily times of prayer and fellowship with God. Ask him to draw close to you as you fellowship with him.

For Your Family and Friends

Pray for any in your circle of Christian friends whose prayer life has grown thin. Ask that they will be reminded that God does hear and answer prayer.

For the Church

Ask God's blessing on the evangelism committee members of your congregation. Pray that they will be effective in helping your church to reach out more.

For the Kingdom

Pray for the work of prayer ministries throughout North America. Pray that they will receive the financial support needed to keep the work of prayer before the church.

For the Unsaved

God has long arms when it comes to salvation. No one is beyond his reach. Thank him for that truth and pray for one unsaved person you know.

Prayer Pointer

"Ministry without prayer becomes work in the power of the flesh. Prayer without ministry is complacent Christianity." —Anonymous

NOVEMBER 29

Personal Prayer

Praise the God who loves even the little children (Lk. 18:16). Give thanks for God's promise in Prov. 22:6 to help parents train their children in the right way. Confess any lack of love or any impatience you have experienced toward your children or others. Commit yourself to a renewed appreciation for the place children have in God's sight. Ask for wisdom to train your children in his ways.

For Your Family and Friends

Pray for the training of covenant children in your congregation. Ask God to bless their nurture at home and in the church. Pray also for their parents.

For the Church

Pray for God's blessing on the children's educational programs in your congregation. Pray for the teachers in the church school and leaders of children's clubs.

For the Kingdom

Ask God to "turn the hearts of the fathers to their children, and the hearts of the children to their fathers" (Mal. 4:6) throughout his kingdom.

For the Unsaved

Pray that people who do not yet trust in Jesus will have a sincere desire to become children of the living God.

NOVEMBER 30

Personal Prayer

Praise the God who knows your sinful ways, but is still there to heal, guide, and comfort you (Isa. 57:18). Give thanks for God's constant faithfulness. Confess any sinful deeds or thoughts that have remained unconfessed. Commit yourself to seeking the guidance of the Holy Spirit every day. Ask him to walk close beside you today.

For Your Family and Friends

Pray for any family member or friend who is in need of God's comfort in a special way. Ask for opportunities to minister his healing grace to them.

For the Church

Pray for God's blessing in worldwide missions. Intercede for missionary families known to you. Pray that they will experience the joy of the harvest. Ask that Satan's schemes may be thwarted.

For the Kingdom

Ask God to expand his kingdom throughout the world as people are brought to him one by one. Pray for a clear sense of God's purpose for you in his kingdom.

For the Unsaved

Pray for an opportunity in the next day to share your faith with someone who does not know Jesus. Ask God to give you courage and boldness in your witness.

Prayer Pointer

"The church's greatest deficiency today is in power—not in programs, strategies, materials, or ideas. And power for ministry can be released only through prayer." —ANONYMOUS

DECEMBER 1

Personal Prayer

Praise God, who is a refuge for the poor and needy (Isa.25:4). Thank him for caring about those who are in desperate circumstances. Confess times when you have not shown compassion to the needy. Commit yourself to serving others in new and stretching ways. Ask God to provide those opportunities for you.

For Your Family and Friends

Thank God for being a shelter from the storm for your family (25:4). Pray that teens will seek that shelter rather than taking refuge in the world.

For the Church

Ask God to anoint the fellowship in your congregation with the Holy Spirit. Pray that any friction between members will be addressed and healed. Pray that newcomers will find a refuge in your congregation.

For the Kingdom

Intercede for ministries which bring Christ's compassion to the poor and needy throughout the world. Ask that their needs will be met as they bring hope to thousands.

For the Unsaved

Pray that one unsaved person you know will see and desire the shelter which Jesus offers. Ask that God will use you to guide that person into eternal safety.

DECEMBER 2

Personal Prayer

Praise God, who is "holy, holy, holy" (Isa. 6:3). Give thanks for God's glory, which is seen throughout the whole earth. Confess any sin which keeps you from experiencing the holiness and glory of God. Commit your life anew today to seeking God's holiness and glory. Ask him to reveal himself to you as you seek his glory in your life.

For Your Family and Friends

Pray that your family will have a renewed sense of God's glory in all areas of your family life—our work, relationships, conversation, leisure time, and so on.

For the Church

Ask God to bless your congregation financially. Pray that members will give like the Macedonians gave to the ministry of the apostle Paul—yond their ability (2 Cor.8:3), but first to the Lord.

For the Kingdom

Pray for all gospel preachers throughout God's kingdom. Ask him to prosper their work as they labor in the harvest field. Pray that the Lord of the harvest will add his blessing to the proclamation of the good news.

For the Unsaved

Pray for any unsaved single parents you may know. Ask God to show you how you can help them in their child rearing. Pray for opportunities to share the gospel of Jesus Christ.

Prayer Pointer

"The ministry of intercession is very demanding. To be serious about intercession is to be ready to give ourselves for the sake of others." —Maxie Dunnam

DECEMBER 3

Personal Prayer

Praise God for his overruling love (2 Cor. 5:14). Give thanks that God's love compels you to do things which please him. Confess those times when you have chosen not to listen to God's words and direction. Commit yourself to worshiping God, for his power over those things that destroy love. Ask God to reveal his overruling love in your daily life.

For Your Family and Friends

Pray that your family and friends will make decisions today which reflect the love of God in their lives.

For the Church

Pray that through the worship of God your church family will be moved to more fully appreciate and experience God's power.

For the Kingdom

Pray that Satan's opposition will be bound so that men and women of all nations will see God's powerful love.

For the Unsaved

Ask that the love of God will compel you to take the risks necessary to share the gospel with someone who has not yet heard.

DECEMBER 4

Personal Prayer

Praise God for his everlasting power and goodness. Thank him for sharing his power with you in Christ. Confess those times when you tend to trust in your own power and strength. Commit yourself to focusing on God's power at work within you. Ask God to fill you with a renewed awareness of his presence within you.

For Your Family and Friends

Pray that your family and friends who know Jesus will seek his power for daily living.

For the Church

Pray that your church leaders will recognize that God's power is greater than that of Satan and act accordingly, knowing they have nothing to fear.

For the Kingdom

Pray that the contrast between good and evil will become very distinct so that God's everlasting power will be made known to all.

For the Unsaved

Ask God to enable you to show unconditional love to people who do not yet know Christ and his everlasting power.

Prayer Pointer

"No day is well spent without communication with God." —Anonymous

DECEMBER 5

Personal Prayer

Praise God for the creativity and imagination with which he has gifted you. Thank him for giving you the desire to live for Christ. Confess those times when you have allowed your thoughts and imagination to stray into sin. Commit yourself to setting your mind on all the fullness of God. Ask God to expand your thoughts of him as you consider the width and depth and breadth of his glory.

For Your Family and Friends

Pray that your family and friends take time to rest from their busy schedules in order to reflect on God's creativity in nature.

For the Church

Pray your church's outreach efforts will also reflect the imagination and creativity of your church members. Ask that the outreach will be effective in reaching your community.

For the Kingdom

Thank God for the beauty of his creation throughout the world. Ask that natural beauty will be protected from the harm which sin inflicts on the creation. Pray that people around the world will see and say, "What an awesome God!"

For the Unsaved

Pray that unsaved people will gain a sense of God's creative power as they consider the complexity of the human body. Ask that such thoughts will lead them to seek the Savior.

DECEMBER 6

Personal Prayer

Praise God as the one who speaks "in your language." Give thanks for God's ongoing communication with you through his Word. Confess the fact that sometimes God speaks, but you disobediently choose not to listen. Commit yourself to the active obedience of young Samuel, who said, "Speak, for your servant is listening" (1 Sam. 3:10). Ask God to give you ears to hear his message.

For Your Family and Friends

Pray that those close to you will also have the desire to listen to God and to obey his Word.

For the Church

Pray that the teachers working in your Christian education program will speak on behalf of God as they teach and apply his Word among students of all ages.

For the Kingdom

Pray for the ministry of gospel broadcasting agencies who use the airwaves to send God's message in many languages throughout the earth.

For the Unsaved

Pray that the contrast between good and evil will be so distinct that even those with the weakest spiritual hearing will hear the good news of Jesus Christ.

Prayer Pointer

"An hour of prayer at the beginning of the [council] meeting actually shortens the overall meeting time by bringing a greater spirit of unity, by emphasizing spiritual priorities, and by opening people's hearts to the Spirit's guidance."
—Anonymous

DECEMBER 7

Personal Prayer

Praise God even in your weakness, believing that in Christ, when you are weak, then you are strong (2 Cor. 12:10). Thank God for opportunities to serve him with perseverance and purpose. Confess those times when you chose to believe that spiritual power comes from within you. Commit yourself to appropriate "boasting" in your weaknesses so that Christ's power might be made even more evident in your life (12:9). Ask God to help you "delight" even in the tough times of life.

For Your Family and Friends

Pray for spiritually and physically weak members of your family or friends. Ask that God's Spirit will empower and strengthen them.

For the Church

Ask the Holy Spirit to empower missionaries who preach and teach the gospel in countries and cultures very different from your own (Acts 1:8).

For the Kingdom

Pray that Christians in every part of the globe will be strengthened to do battle with the evil spiritual forces that are at work in our world. Pray for an outpouring of God's power throughout his church worldwide.

For the Unsaved

Pray that the life-giving power of Jesus Christ will be revealed to unsaved people you know. Pray for them by name.

DECEMBER 8

Personal Prayer

Praise God for confiding in those who love him (Ps. 25:14). Give thanks for this developing relationship God has established with you. Confess those times when you have refused to share intimately with God. Commit yourself to seeking his companionship daily. Ask God to create within you a desire for intimacy, total honesty, acceptance, and joy in his presence.

For Your Family and Friends

Pray that God will bring fulfillment to those who are suffering from the pain of unfulfilled dreams.

For the Church

Pray that true intimacy will be demonstrated by the children of God in a way that is appealing and attractive to unbelievers who are observing.

For the Kingdom

Pray that those who have suffered sexual, emotional, and/or physical abuse will be helped to understand and experience intimacy.

For the Unsaved

Ask God to give you the opportunity and courage to befriend a person seeking a meaningful friendship. Ask that Jesus will be the center of your relationship.

Prayer Pointer

"It is not possible to explain the power and effectiveness of the New Testament church without reference to prayer." —ANONYMOUS

DECEMBER 9

Personal Prayer

Praise the God who lays claim to the entire world and all that live in it (Ps. 24:1). Thank him for the food, shelter, and clothing that sustains you and gives comfort to your life. Confess the times when you have failed to acknowledge God's riches in your life. Commit yourself to examining your acts of stewardship. Ask God to give you a heart of liberality, knowing that all you have comes from him (1 Chron. 29:14).

For Your Family and Friends

Ask God to show your family new and creative ways to share the abundance of your lives with families who have much less.

For the Church

Pray that your church will take seriously the stewardship of God's resources. Pray for those who make decisions regarding finances in your church. Ask for wisdom.

For the Kingdom

Ask God's blessing among Christian communities where there is poverty, hunger, and deprivation. Pray for justice where there is economic injustice.

For the Unsaved

Pray that your own giving spirit toward others will speak volumes concerning Christ's generous gift of salvation to all who believe.

DECEMBER 10

Personal Prayer

Praise God for the diversity of his creation. Give thanks for your heritage and unique attributes which add to the abundance of God's diverse creation. Confess those times when you failed to accept and love people unlike yourself. Commit yourself to learning about and thanking God for other cultures. Ask God to stretch your understanding of who he is and what he desires of you.

For Your Family and Friends

Praise God for each family member and friend. They are so different in personality. Thank God for their diversity.

For the Church

As you worship God this Sunday, take a mental tour of the pews near you. Silently pray for the people sitting in those pews. Again thank God for their diversity—and for your church's unity.

For the Kingdom

Pray that cultural diversity will be recognized as a gift of God.

For the Unsaved

Ask God to open doors of opportunity for you to share the gospel with someone from a differing background or culture. Pray that God will prepare you for that divine encounter this week.

Prayer Pointer

"God's power enters our human programs through the door of prayer. Unless the church's ministry is bathed in prayer, it remains merely a human endeavor."
—Anonymous

DECEMBER 11

Personal Prayer

Praise God for his marvelous plan of redemption worked out through history. Thank God for the significant leaders he called to make a difference in the growth of the Christian movement. Confess times when God called you to lead in some way, but you chose rather to follow. Commit yourself to discovering how the use of your gifts can influence others to follow Jesus. Ask God to give you courage and insight as he calls you to go and bear fruit that will last (Jn. 15:16).

For Your Family and Friends

Pray that your family members and friends will recognize and use their gifts for the growth of God's kingdom.

For the Church

Pray that leaders in your church will have the burden and ability to seek and disciple others.

For the Kingdom

Pray that political leaders throughout the world will recognize Jesus Christ as Lord. Ask that repentance and revival will come to nations which have not yet honored him.

For the Unsaved

Pray that gang leaders will see their influence transformed to a positive affect. Pray that their desire for control and acceptance will be satisfied through the power and blood of Jesus Christ. Pray that God will give them a vision for their potential to lead a broken generation.

DECEMBER 12

Personal Prayer

Praise God for caring for you (1 Pet. 5:7). Thank him for being so interested in your welfare that he even knows the number of hairs on your head (Lk. 12:7). Confess those times when you failed to take his care seriously. Commit yourself to imitating God's care by caring selflessly for others. Ask him to fill your heart and mind with a sense of his deep love for you.

For Your Family and Friends

Thank God for those who reach out to you with acts of kindness. Thank him for acts of kindness shown by members of your own family.

For the Church

Pray that your church's evangelistic efforts will be caring efforts. Ask God to show your church how to minister to more than just the spiritual needs of those who don't have a saving relationship with Christ.

For the Kingdom

Pray that communication specialists throughout the world will work together to increase opportunities for thousands of people to learn about Jesus.

For the Unsaved

Ask God to help you show a sincere, caring attitude toward one unsaved person today. Look for opportunities to share the gospel with that person.

Prayer Pointer

"Life's best outlook is a prayerful uplook." —Anonymous

DECEMBER 13

Personal Prayer

Pray Daniel's words of praise: "Praise be to the name of God for ever and ever; wisdom and power are his" (Dan. 2:20). Thank God for guiding you to make wise choices in life. Confess times when you chose to follow the foolishness of this world's wisdom rather than the wisdom of God. Commit yourself to seeking the "Spirit of wisdom and of understanding" (Isa. 11:2). Ask God to give to you the "wisdom that comes from heaven" (Jas. 3:17).

For Your Family and Friends

Pray for students among your family and friends. Ask that they will gain knowledge in their studies, but more, that they will gain the wisdom which comes from trusting in the Lord (Job 28:28).

For the Church

Pray that your church's education program will focus on matters of the heart as well as of the head.

For the Kingdom

Ask God's blessing on Christian scientists as they explore the mysteries of God's wisdom displayed in the natural realm. Ask that God's clear fingerprints will be seen in all their experiments and discoveries.

For the Unsaved

Pray for the ability to keep your testimony simple and genuine as you cross paths with people who are trying to understand the things of God.

DECEMBER 14

Personal Prayer

Praise God for choosing you "before the creation of the world to be holy and blameless in his sight" (Eph. 1:4). Thank him for choosing the poor in the world's eyes to be rich in faith (Jas. 2:5). Confess the times when you have felt apathetic toward God's lordship. Commit yourself to living in his promises as revealed in the Word. Ask God to help you live a holy and blameless life.

For Your Family and Friends

Thank God for ancestors who loved the Lord and passed down the stories of the Christian faith to their children and grandchildren. Pray that you will do the same in your family.

For the Church

Ask God to prosper the work of world missionaries which your church supports. Pray for them and their families by name.

For the Kingdom

Pray for aviation and transportation agencies which support the work of the gospel overseas. Ask for personal safety and the financial resources needed to carry on their ministries.

For the Unsaved

Pray for the advance of the gospel among the baby boomer generation. Ask that they will find the answer to their desire for purposeful living in Jesus Christ.

Prayer Pointer

"It is in private prayer that we most easily get in touch with our spiritual selves."
—Anonymous

DECEMBER 15

Personal Prayer

As you praise God today, focus on his great mercy (Ps. 108:4). Thank him for taking delight in surrounding you with his mercy (Mic. 7:18). Confess that in the busyness of life you sometimes forget his mercy to you. Commit yourself to extending that same kind of loving mercy to others who are in need. Ask God to grant you his peace and fellowship as you live for him this day.

For Your Family and Friends

Thank God for showing his mercy to your family. Pray that any unbelieving family members will turn from sin to the Lord.

For the Church

Pray that your church will also extend God's mercy to the needy and impoverished members of your community. Ask that God will open eyes to see opportunities for service.

For the Kingdom

Ask that the church will increasingly become a haven of hope and healing for some who seek answers only in the psychiatrist's office.

For the Unsaved

Pray that unsaved people you know will discover that God really is full of mercy, and that that is what they ultimately need!

DECEMBER 16

Personal Prayer

Praise God, who is the creator of both rich and poor. Thank him for giving you the ability to produce wealth (Deut. 8:18). Confess any time you have put your trust in your earthly possessions rather than in the spiritual riches of God (8:13-14). Commit yourself to living contentedly with all that God has provided. Ask him to give you a generous heart toward those who have less.

For Your Family and Friends

Pray that God will meet physical and financial needs among your family members and friends. Pray for opportunities to give what you can to meet their need.

For the Church

Pray that God will add his blessing to the stewardship of your congregation. Pray also for the wise distribution of funds to meet various needs.

For the Kingdom

Ask God to open the pocketbooks of church members worldwide. Pray that there will be an outpouring of generosity equal to that of the Macedonian Christians (2 Cor. 8:2) in Paul's day.

For the Unsaved

Pray that unsaved people will view believers as unselfish and giving. Ask that they will be drawn to Christ as they observe selfless acts of service.

Prayer Pointer

"If I could hear Christ praying for me in the next room, I would not fear a million enemies. Yet distance makes no difference. He is praying for me."
—Robert Murray McCheyne

DECEMBER 17

Personal Prayer

Praise the God of truth, whose words are trustworthy (2 Sam. 7:28). Thank Jesus for being the only way, truth, and life (Jn. 14:6). Confess the times you've chosen to believe the lies of Satan rather than the true promises of God. Commit yourself, as a member of Christ's body, to speaking truthfully in all your relationships (Eph. 4:25). Ask God to buckle the belt of truth around your waist.

For Your Family and Friends

The Bible says that God detests lying lips (Prov. 12:22). Ask God to guard the lips of you and your children at home, school, and work.

For the Church

As you gather for worship this week, pray that the one who brings God's message will set "forth the truth plainly" and not "distort the word of God" (2 Cor. 4:2).

For the Kingdom

Pray that truth will be honored by your local government officials—supervisors, mayors, commissioners, judges. Ask that they will be committed wholeheartedly to advancing truth in the public square (Zech. 8:16).

For the Unsaved

The devil is "a liar and the father of lies" (Jn. 8:44). Ask that Satan's empty schemes will be exposed and that unsaved people will believe in Jesus.

DECEMBER 18

Personal Prayer

Praise your God, whose right hand is filled with righteousness (Ps. 48:10). Thank him for being righteous in all his ways and loving toward all he has made (Ps. 145:17). Confess your own sinfulness, especially times in the last day when you have acted in an unrighteous way toward others. Commit yourself to being "filled with the fruit of righteousness that comes through Jesus Christ" (Phil. 1:11). Ask God to keep you in close communion with him throughout this day.

For Your Family and Friends

Ask God to enable believing teens among your family and friends to "say 'No' to ungodliness and worldly passions, and to live self-controlled, upright and godly lives" (Titus 2:12).

For the Church

Pray for the elders of your congregation by name. Ask God that they will be models of right living for your congregation.

For the Kingdom

Pray for all efforts to bring godliness and righteousness to the great institutions of our society. Intercede for Christian leaders in business, education, and government.

For the Unsaved

Ask God to touch the hearts of unbelievers who are living for themselves, that they will come to their senses and stop sinning (1 Cor. 15:34).

DECEMBER 19

Personal Prayer

Praise God who has invited you into his circle of fellowship through Jesus Christ. Thank him for his invitation to love him with your whole being (Mk. 12:33). Confess to God that sometimes you don't love and honor him as you should. Commit yourself to Deut. 10:12: "To fear the LORD your God, to walk in his ways, to love him, and to serve [him] with all your heart and with all your soul." Ask God to enable you fulfill that commitment today.

For Your Family and Friends

Think of the oldest and the youngest members of your family. Ask God to meet the special needs of those two people. Thank God that his love spans many generations.

For the Church

Pray that the evangelistic outreach of your church will be driven simply by a genuine love for people. Ask that any pride or self-will will be confessed.

For the Kingdom

Pray that the knowledge of Christ will spread throughout the whole world, even as a tiny seed grows into a large and vigorous plant (Mk. 4:31). Pray for faithful preachers of the gospel (Mt. 24:14).

For the Unsaved

Ask God to make you more alert to the needs of unsaved people you know. Pray that God will show you practical ways you can minister to them and ultimately show them how to believe.

DECEMBER 20

Personal Prayer

Praise God for the humility which Christ displayed in coming to earth and going to the cross for you (Phil. 2:8). Thank Jesus for modeling true humility as he washed his disciples' feet (Jn. 13:5). Confess the pride which keeps you from wholeheartedly submitting to Jesus' lordship. Commit yourself to drawing near to your Lord at the foot of the cross. Ask him to give you a servant's heart.

For Your Family and Friends

Pray that God will give you opportunities this week to serve those close to you. Ask that all your actions will be fueled by humility and not false pride.

For the Church

Thank God for the teachers in your church's adult education program. Give thanks also for curriculum materials and Christian publishers who provide quality instructional materials.

For the Kingdom

Ask for God's blessing on Christian artists and musicians who bring praise and glory to God through their creative expressions.

For the Unsaved

Ask God to search your heart concerning unsaved persons you know. Pray that any attitude of superiority will be rooted out of your life so that you can humbly and genuinely present the claims of Christ.

Prayer Pointer

"Any church without a well-organized and systematic prayer program is simply operating a religious treadmill." —John Billheimer

DECEMBER 21

Personal Prayer

Praise the God of faith, hope, and love (1 Cor. 13:13). Thank him for the "new birth into a living hope through the resurrection of Jesus Christ" (1 Pet. 1:3). Confess those times when you have given in to discouragement rather than hoping in God. Commit yourself to taking hold of the hope which God freely offers to you (Heb. 6:18). Ask that you will have opportunity to share your hope with another person today.

For Your Family and Friends

Pray for any member of your family who is downcast and despairing. Ask that the God of hope will bring a measure of comfort and peace.

For the Church

Pray for missionaries by name who serve in other countries. Ask God to bless their labors, to spare them from discouragement, and to remind them of many reasons to hope in God.

For the Kingdom

Ask God's anointing of Christians who bring Jesus' comfort and peace to those afflicted with terminal illnesses. Pray for those ministering in Christ's name to people suffering from the effects of AIDS.

For the Unsaved

Ask God to help you live in such a way that your unsaved friends will ask "you to give the reason for the hope that you have" (1 Pet. 3:15). Then be ready with your answer!

DECEMBER 22

Personal Prayer

Praise your God, who alone is holy (Rev. 15:4). Thank him for the glorious promise that one day all nations will come and worship him. Confess sins which keep you from drawing close to God. Commit yourself daily to exalting and worshiping your holy God. Ask God to help you keep his command to "be holy, because I am holy" (Lev. 11:45).

For Your Family and Friends

In all your family relationships, pray that the truth of Heb. 12:14 will be central: "Make every effort to live in peace with all men and to be holy."

For the Church

Pray that the members of your congregation will welcome guests to your church with warmth and hospitality. Ask God to remove apathy and indifference.

For the Kingdom

Pray that believers throughout the world will conform their wills to God in order to "live holy and godly lives" (2 Pet. 3:11).

For the Unsaved

Pray that unsaved people you know will be drawn to Jesus because of the attractiveness of your holy living.

Prayer Pointer

"If family worship is neglected, other attempts at prayer are like sprinkling the foliage of a plant while leaving the roots dry." —Anonymous

DECEMBER 23

Personal Prayer

Praise "the Father of the heavenly lights, who does not change like shifting shadows" (Jas. 1:17). Thank God for remaining the same throughout all eternity (Ps. 102:27). Confess that sometimes you are not as consistent as you would like to be in your walk with God. Commit yourself to remaining true to that which does not change, the eternal God (2 Cor. 4:18). Ask God to glorify himself in your life.

For Your Family and Friends

Pray that in the midst of life's many changes, those closest to you will remain true to God and his Word. Pray for balance and harmony in each life.

For the Church

Pray that the stewardship of resources in your congregation will please God. Ask that members will be willing to give generously of their time and talents as well as their finances. Pray that they will experience joy in giving.

For the Kingdom

Ask God to change the hearts of men and women and children who hear the good news spoken by evangelists around the world. Pray for a great worldwide harvest of souls this year.

For the Unsaved

Pray for God to open your eyes to one person who needs the gospel. Prepare your heart by asking God to give you the words to say and the confidence to say them when God opens the door.

DECEMBER 24

Personal Prayer

Focus on Jn. 15:1-17 for the next few days. Praise your Father, who is the gardener of your soul. Thank Jesus for being the true vine which nourishes and gives life to the branches. Confess moments when you've tried to sever your relationship to Jesus in some way. Commit yourself to welcoming God's pruning in your life despite the pain it might bring. Ask God to make you more fruitful as you live for him.

For Your Family and Friends

Ask God to make the "garden" of your family members a fruitful and abundant place. Pray for his tilling and planting and nurturing of faith among those close to you.

For the Church

Ask the true vine to take root in every family represented in your home church. Pray that the joy of union with Christ will be evident in your worship.

For the Kingdom

Pray that the true vine will flourish throughout the world, as Jesus draws people of every nation to himself in repentance and faith.

For the Unsaved

Ask that your fruit-bearing will be attractive to unsaved people you know. Pray that they will "taste [of that fruit] and see that the LORD is good" (Ps. 34:8).

Prayer Pointer

"God rules the world through the prayers of his people." —ANONYMOUS

DECEMBER 25

Personal Prayer

Praise Jesus, the true vine, for the privilege of being one of his branches. Thank him for the promise of union with himself (Jn. 15:4). Confess the times when you have proudly thought of yourself as the vine rather than as a branch. Commit yourself to remaining in the true vine. Ask God to keep you firmly attached to the vine so that you can bear much fruit.

For Your Family and Friends

Pray for childless friends who desire to have children. Ask God to give them this desire of their heart. Pray that they will have patience to wait on the Lord and to submit to his timing.

For the Church

Pray that the leaders of your congregation will be fruit-bearing branches. Pray that a vital union with Christ will be evident in the lives of elders, deacons, and other church leaders.

For the Kingdom

Ask God to bless the fellowship of local church bodies where members are challenged to "remain in Christ." Pray for unity among such Christians in neighborhoods and communities around the world.

For the Unsaved

Pray that your wholehearted commitment to Christ will be attractive to one unsaved person you know. Ask God to give you an opportunity to share your faith with that person.

DECEMBER 26

Personal Prayer

Praise God as the one who makes it possible for you to bear much fruit (Jn. 15:5). Thank him for the promise of a great spiritual harvest in your life. Confess sins which stunt the development of spiritual fruit in your life. Commit yourself to daily devotional habits which will stimulate the growth of such fruit. Ask God to help you produce the kind of harvest which will give him the glory and praise.

For Your Family and Friends

Pray that the teenagers in your family or among your friends will commit themselves to being fruit-bearing young people. Pray that they will learn that "apart from [Jesus, they] can do nothing" (15:5).

For the Church

Pray for fruitfulness in the evangelistic efforts of your congregation. Ask that an increasing number of members will join in "seeking the lost" in your neighborhood. Pray for the outreach leaders.

For the Kingdom

Ask God to pour out his blessing on his church throughout the world. Pray for fruitfulness among those who remain faithful to God and are firmly united to Jesus, the true vine.

For the Unsaved

Pray by name for any unsaved friends in your work place or neighborhood. Pray that they will have the courage to ask you about your faith. Ask God to prepare you for that conversation.

DECEMBER 27

Personal Prayer

Praise your God, who is the giver of all good gifts (Mt. 7:11). Thank him for his promise to give you "whatever you wish" (Jn. 15:7) if you remain in him. Confess times when you have failed to thank God for his many spiritual and temporal gifts to you. Commit yourself to imitating God's generosity as you give to others and to God. Ask him to help you freely give as you have freely received (Mt. 10:8).

For Your Family and Friends

Pray that parents of small children will give of their time to their children while they are young. Ask that family time will be viewed as a sacred trust and not as a burden.

For the Church

Thank God for the teachers in your church's adult education program. Pray that they will have a sense of God's call to this important work. Ask that they will be firmly united to Christ.

For the Kingdom

Pray for colleges and universities around the world which honor the name of Christ in their education. Ask God to prosper their influence in the lives of thousands of students worldwide.

For the Unsaved

Ask God to use you to lead a person to the most important gift of God, which is eternal life through Jesus Christ (Rom. 6:23).

DECEMBER 28

Personal Prayer

Praise Jesus for the depth of his redeeming love, which sent him to the cross for you (Gal. 2:20). Thank him for dying on your behalf. Confess any lack of love you feel toward a brother or sister. Commit yourself to remaining in Jesus' love by keeping his commandments (Jn. 15:10). Ask God to show his love to you in new ways today.

For Your Family and Friends

Ask for God's love to permeate all of your relationships with other family members and friends. Pray that Jesus' peace will heal any tension or discord in those relationships.

For the Church

Pray that world missionary organizations will be effective in preaching and teaching the love of God in Christ to people who have never heard the gospel before. Ask that the mission personnel will be "rooted and established in love" (Eph. 3:17).

For the Kingdom

Pray that all of God's children throughout his kingdom will exult in the great love which God has lavished on those who believe (1 Jn. 3:1).

For the Unsaved

Ask that the redeeming love of God will come gently to an unsaved person you know. Ask God to reveal a glimpse of his unconditional love through you.

Prayer Pointer

"Nothing lies beyond the reach of prayer except that which lies beyond the will of God." —ANONYMOUS

DECEMBER 29

Personal Prayer

Praise God that the Christian life includes periods of "complete" and unbridled joy (Jn. 15:11). Thank Jesus for being your joy-filled Savior (Lk. 10:21). Confess any sin that stands in the way of your experiencing the fullness of joy which Jesus provides. Commit yourself today to rejoicing in the Lord, to being joyful in God your Savior (Hab. 3:18). Ask Jesus to make his joy in you complete.

For Your Family and Friends

Is there joy in your home? Ask God to show you ways you can bring joy to others in your family or to your friends. Pray for a joyful spirit as you think creatively.

For the Church

Ask that joy will characterize the fellowship of your congregation. Pray that it will flow out to embrace those on the edges of your church who are hurting or wandering.

For the Kingdom

Thank God that his kingdom is full of "righteousness, peace and joy in the Holy Spirit" (Rom. 14:17). Commit yourself to being a joyful citizen of that kingdom in all that you do.

For the Unsaved

Pray that the joy which Christ offers will attract many whose unconfessed sin keeps them in sadness and despair.

DECEMBER 30

Personal Prayer

Praise Jesus for calling you his friend (Jn. 15:15). Thank him for giving you a job to do in his kingdom—that is, to "bear fruit" (15:16). Confess those times when you've sought to do your own work rather than God's work. Commit yourself to bearing fruit that will last. Ask Jesus for the strength and wisdom you need to carry out his commands.

For Your Family and Friends

Praise God for family members and friends who also have been called by him to bear fruit. Thank Jesus for his friendship with them. Pray that they will seek to nurture that friendship with their Savior.

For the Church

Pray that the friends of God in your church will be generous in their financial contributions to his work. Pray that ministries of your congregation will not suffer from lack of funds.

For the Kingdom

Ask that Jesus' appointing of his disciples to "go and bear fruit" will capture the hearts and minds of Christians worldwide. Ask God what part you can play in his plan of fruit-bearing.

For the Unsaved

Pray that Jesus, who was called a "friend of . . . sinners" (Mt. 11:19), will befriend an unsaved person you know. Ask Jesus how you, too, might become a friend of sinners in order that they might come to Christ in faith.

DECEMBER 31

Personal Prayer

As you come to the end of the year, lift your voice in praise to the one who is a prayer-hearing and prayer-answering God. Thank him for the tender talks you have had with him over the past year. Confess those times when you foolishly doubted the power of prayer. Commit yourself to maintaining a daily prayer time in the coming year. Ask God to keep you accountable to him.

For Your Family and Friends

Take a few moments to recount all the blessings your family has enjoyed over the past year. Thank God for those. Recall also the sorrows. Pray for anyone who is still hurting.

For the Church

Thank God for your local church, especially for numerical and spiritual growth among members. Pray for peace in your church in the coming year. Ask God's blessing on your pastor and other leaders.

For the Kingdom

Pray for God's kingdom to come in the coming year. Ask that believers throughout the earth will be bold witnesses for Christ so that all people everywhere might have the opportunity to hear the gospel.

For the Unsaved

Ask God to bring in any unsaved friend or family member who yet remains outside of Christ. Give thanks for wandering sheep he has rescued in this past year.